W9-BTP-885

·1989·
Country Home.
Collection

© Copyright 1989 by Meredith Corporation, Des Moines, Iowa.
All Rights Reserved. Printed in the United States of America.
First Edition. First Printing.
ISSN: 1040-7235
ISBN: 0-696-01874-8

Country Home.

Editor: Jean LemMon
Managing Editor: Ann Omvig Manternach
Art Director: Jill M. Carey

Senior Features and Building Editor: John Riha
Home Furnishings Editor: Candace Ord Manroe
Interior Design Editor: Joseph Boehm
Food and Garden Editor: Molly Culbertson
Antiques and Collectibles Editor: Linda Joan Smith
Assistant Art Director: Stan Sams
Associate Features Editor: Beverly Brown
Copy Chief: Mike Maine
Copy Editors: Joe Hawkins, Michelle Sillman
Administrative Assistant: Becky A. Brame

Contributing Editors
Barbara Cathcart, Karol K. DeWulf, Eileen A. Deymier,
Estelle Bond Guralnick, Deborah Hufford, Ellen Kaye,
Marcia King, Ruth L. Reiter, Mary Anne Thomson, Pamela Wilson
American Style: Virginia & Lee McAlester
Historic House Update: Michael Leccese
Old Home Place: Katherine M. Knight
View from a Country Kitchen: Pauline Wanderer

Publisher: Jerry Kaplan
Vice President/Publishing Director: Adolph Auerbacher
Vice President/Operations: Dean Pieters

BETTER HOMES AND GARDENS® BOOKS
Editor: Gerald M. Knox
Art Director: Ernest Shelton
Managing Editor: David A. Kirchner

President, Book Group: Jeramy Lanigan
Vice President, Retail Marketing: Jamie L. Martin
Vice President, Administrative Services: Rick Rundall

BETTER HOMES AND GARDENS® MAGAZINE
President, Magazine Group: James A. Autry
Editorial Director: Doris Eby
Editorial Services Director: Duane L. Gregg

MEREDITH CORPORATION OFFICERS
Chairman of the Executive Committee: E. T. Meredith III
Chairman of the Board: Robert A. Burnett
President: Jack D. Rehm

1989 COUNTRY HOME® COLLECTION
Editor: Jean LemMon
Editorial Project Manager: Marsha Jahns
Graphic Designer: Mary Schlueter Bendgen
Electronic Text Processor: Paula Forest
Contributing Project Editor: Mary Helen Schiltz

Contents

Country homes exude
a timeless beauty and craftsmanship all their own.
And every other month, COUNTRY HOME®
magazine publishes outstanding
examples of America's lovingly restored, beautifully decorated country houses. Now, in the
1989 COUNTRY HOME® COLLECTION, you can
rediscover 17 of the most memorable country
homes published by COUNTRY HOME®
magazine in 1988. This yearbook celebrates the
individuality of country living and decorating,
featuring all kinds of country homes, from a brand-
new storybook home and a seaside cottage,
to a grand old house built in the 1800s and a
pioneer cabin set amid gently rolling hills. Walk
with us now through these pages and into the
homes and lives of those who have been inspired by
a love of the country life-style.

February

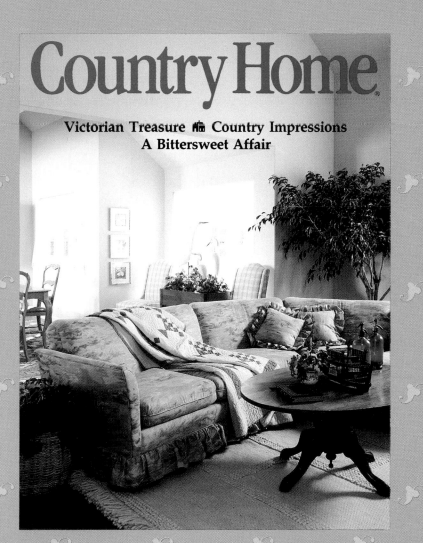

Country Home

Victorian Treasure 🏠 Country Impressions
A Bittersweet Affair

VICTORIAN TREASURE

The Saia family worked hard to uncover the charm hidden in a dilapidated seaside cottage.

By Linda Joan Smith

Like a beached ship that has sailed its last voyage and lies ungainly upon the shore, this vintage summer home once languished at the mercy of the sun, sea winds, and modern-day marauders. It was scheduled for demolition when Sal and Mary Jane Saia, long-time vacationers on New Jersey's Long Beach Island, stumbled upon its tarnished charms at the close of the summer in 1984.

"We had a ritual each rainy day," says Mary Jane, whose interest in the preservation of historic buildings goes back many years. "We'd traipse off to the local Realtor's office and ask what kinds of homes were available on the island that fit both our budget and my fantasies." Those two criteria didn't coincide until a drizzly day four years ago, just before the Saias were leaving the slender island to return to their home in northern New Jersey.

"The real estate agent mentioned he had this house that was going to be knocked down if the bank couldn't find a buyer," says Mary Jane. "He indicated it was an

Left *and* above: *The sirens of the sea can be heard from the porch of this once-abandoned summer home, which is now reliving the glory days of its Victorian youth.*
Top: *Sal and Mary Jane Saia rescued the foundering house in 1984 and embarked on a challenging voyage of restoration.*

Photographs: Maris/Semel. Field editor: Eileen A. Deymier

VICTORIAN TREASURE

old, dilapidated thing, one we certainly wouldn't be interested in. He was reluctant, but we finally talked him into showing it to us."

Mary Jane recalls that initial visit with a satisfied smile. "When we arrived, the place was totally overgrown with shrubs, and there were flocks of pigeons—and piles of their droppings—on the roof and porch. The steps were off, and there was a gaping hole in the porch where the boards had rotted out. There were windows broken and the house had been vandalized many, many times." In spite of the disastrous appearance of the place, Sal, who had previously built his family one house and was in the process of restoring another, could tell the old cottage was structurally sound.

For the Saias, buying the dilapidated house was a fitting expression of their fondness for the town of Barnegat Light, their love of long walks on the beach, and their passion for old homes.

"Barnegat Light has one of the most wonderful beaches anywhere," explains Mary Jane. "And the town itself is natural and unaffected, which we thoroughly enjoy." The time they spend there is a pleasant break both for Sal, who is a physics teacher, and Mary Jane, who is the director of the Family Life office for the Diocese of Paterson, New Jersey.

The Saias began the challenging process of bringing the old house back to life in late 1984 and completed the main portion of the work in August 1985. "Our youngest

Above *and* right: *In choosing the pale colors for the downstairs, Mary Jane says, "I wanted to capture the feeling of the seashore—the water, sand, and sunrises." Light and airy as the foam that rides the whitecaps, much of the wicker furniture was found in the house.*

VICTORIAN TREASURE

son, Timothy, who is in law school, had the summer off and is keenly interested in historic preservation and antiques," says Mary Jane. "So, the three of us made up the body of the work force." They replaced long lost shingles and balusters, repainted peeling walls, shored up the sagging porch roof, restored broken windows and fallen shutters, and carted out loads of garbage and debris.

As they worked, the rooms began to reveal their special treasures. Until Mary Jane and Sal bought the house, it had always been in the same family. Much to the Saias' delight, underneath the clutter that was left behind they found many salvageable items that had belonged to the original owners: a number of wicker pieces, a dining room table and six wooden chairs, an oak washstand, an antique lace slip, a turn-of-the-century watercolor of Barnegat Light. Most of the furniture required refinishing or repainting (the wicker had all been painted black), but now is a cherished reminder of the heritage of this seaside home.

The Saias met their greatest challenge in the kitchen,

Above: *A vivid imagination was required to see beyond the rotten flooring, yellow plastic wall tile, and warped plywood cabinets in the 1950s-era kitchen.*
Right: *The Saias discovered the dining room table and six matching chairs amid the clutter that filled the rooms.*

VICTORIAN TREASURE

which had last undergone a remodeling in the early 1950s and suffered badly during the time the house stood empty. During that remodeling, an unnecessary stairwell had been sealed off but left in place. Sal and Mary Jane removed the stairway to increase their elbowroom, then stripped the room of its peeling flooring, plastic wall tiles, and 1950s plywood cabinetry. Sal built the new cabinets and put in the wainscoting. Old-fashioned glass cabinet doors came from their oldest son's home in northern New Jersey, where they had been set aside during an earlier remodeling.

The old house now welcomes the Saias each year with open arms. But the couple's work is far from done. Along with a love for their own home, Sal and Mary Jane share a deep concern for preserving and perpetuating the charm and history of the town of Barnegat Light—not an easy task in the face of unrelenting pressure from developers and annual damage to the beach and buildings from the ocean's winter fury.

"We fell in love with a typical seaside fishing village of the Victorian Era," says Mary Jane. "We want to help it stay that way." □

Above: *This under-eaves attic bedroom was once used as a storeroom for traveling trunks and old clothes.*
Right: *The master bedroom of the seaside cottage was plagued with broken windows, missing moldings, cracked walls, and a collapsing ceiling. Now it's an airy summertime retreat.*

"Camille Monet and a Child in the Artist's Garden at Argenteuil." Courtesy Museum of Fine Arts, Boston

Country IMPRESSIONS

By Karol K. DeWulf

Abandoning their studios to paint in the outdoors, impressionist artists captured nature's ever-changing show of light and color on canvas during the mid-1800s. Today, the iridescent hues and spontaneous brushstrokes of their work inspire Country Home *magazine's artful creation of impressionistic country interiors.*

Above: *Claude Monet painted his wife and child in their Giverny, France, garden using dots and dashes of color.* Far left: *A painterly fabric (inset,* left) *echoing Monet's style is the sparkling starting point for this inviting breakfast nook. The print, which is stitched into cushions for the pine settee and wicker chairs, is complemented by an Amish-style rag rug.*

Paintings: Claude Monet. Photographs: Tommy Miyasaki, De Gennaro Studios. Architect: Ruscitto/Latham/Blanton
Interior design: Karol K. DeWulf

COUNTRY IMPRESSIONS

Monet's "Water Lilies" exemplifies the impressionistic style of capturing nature's changing beauty in spots of color.

"Water Lilies." The Cleveland Museum of Art
Purchase from the John L. Severance Fund

French painter Claude Monet and his fellow impressionists were haunted by the desire to depict the fleeting moment . . . one's first impression of a scene. Traveling the countryside and painting in the open air, they strove to commit the essence of instantaneous light and color to canvas.

Today, in a French-inspired home set against a backdrop of Idaho's Sawtooth Mountains, *Country Home* magazine translates the shimmering colors and textures of these paintings into room designs reminiscent of French country but bristling with American vitality. Furniture dressed with painterly fabrics in livelier hues and patterns than previously seen in country interiors is arranged against a background of white—echoing the impressionists' sense of space and outdoors for a lighter, fresher country look.

For example, the living room, *left*, is imbued with the illusionary quality of Monet's famous "Water Lilies" series by selecting a fabric inspired by and named for the paintings as a starting point. By covering the sectional sofa, a

Far left: *Liberal use of an impressionistic fabric (inset, above left) sets a serene mood in the living room, while elements such as a plaid clad wing chair and contemporary folk art add country flavor.*
Left: *Idaho's Sawtooth Mountains are a fitting backdrop for the home's French-inspired architecture.*

Upholstery by Pennsylvania House. Sofa fabric by Lee Jofa

COUNTRY IMPRESSIONS

The impressionists painted everyday scenes, creating drama with unusual viewpoints and radiant color.

"Woman with a Parasol—Madame Monet and Her Son." National Gallery of Art, Washington, D.C. Collection of Mr. and Mrs. Paul Mellon

lounge chair, and an ottoman in the softly hued fabric, the pattern's influence is complete.

Contrasting the fabric's grayed purples and greens are splashes of yellow. A flat-woven rug provides a glow underfoot, while potted plants with golden blossoms and a yellow-and-purple quilt are poignant dashes of the eye-catching hue.

In addition to their use of color, the impressionists introduced new and, at the time, revolutionary ideas to the art arena. Contrary to classical teachings, their compositions often were asymmetrical, focusing on segments of a scene rather than its entirety.

In this same spirit, sections of rooms can take on their own composition and mood. The inviting corner, *far right,* is part of a spacious living room but maintains a singular sense of comfort

Far right: *A slice of the living room takes on its own composition: Vertical elegance created by the mirror and lamps is balanced by a horizontal casualness of the chair and folk art swan. The impressionistic paintings are contemporary works.*
Right: *A view toward the sectional sofa reveals a glimpse of the adjacent dining area.*

Commode, mirror, and upholstery by Pennsylvania House. Patterned fabric by Lee Jofa

COUNTRY IMPRESSIONS

The impressionists worshiped light and celebrated its power as a visual tool in their art. The clear light of the French Riviera moved Monet to paint high-keyed canvases of the mountainous seashore.

"Cap Martin, near Menton." Courtesy Museum of Fine Arts, Boston. Juliana Cheney Edwards Collection

and style. Sink-in seating (combined with nearby objects pleasing to both eye and touch) is key to the vignette's success. Paintings of the Idaho countryside, being impressionistic in style, possess a quiet romance.

Impressionists also were in love with light. Monet's paintings pulsated with a sense of inner luminance, directly reflecting the artist's awareness of how light affects color and form. He was known to sit for hours, waiting for the right light to paint his subjects.

Airy, bright interior spaces like the dining room, *left*, also revel in the power of light. Natural lumination from the windows and French doors is intensified by white-painted walls and white lace curtains. In the window's natural light, a trio of egrets is a harmony of white-on-white silhouettes.

Far left: *Country French-style furnishings add a warm glow to the mood of the light-filled dining room. The pieces' soft curves and fanciful carving lend a touch of elegance, while their honey-toned finish keeps them in the country motif.* Left: *A French cheese-drying rack is put to new use as a flower-lined nest for egrets.*

Dining room table and chairs by Pennsylvania House. Plaid fabric by Westgate

COUNTRY IMPRESSIONS

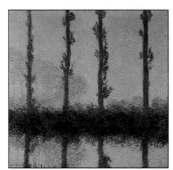

Although not romantic in the classical sense, impressionistic paintings are emotional. Monet's mosaic coloration and depiction of light transform even a stand of poplars into a touching scene.

"The Four Poplars." The Metropolitan Musem of Art, New York. The H. O. Havemeyer Collection

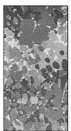

Although time has rendered the subjects of many impressionistic paintings romantic, it hasn't veiled the impressionistic palette with the same nostalgia. Monet's paintings depict typical scenes from the 1800s, but their colors communicate to every generation.

Timeless without being tired, impressionistic colors can inspire beautiful room schemes like the bedroom, *left* and *below.* A painterly fabric in spry greens, blues, and yellows that Monet might have used is the impetus of the appealing retreat. Quilts, a contemporary painting of a country scene, and a needlepoint rug repeat the color melody of the print. Shapely upholstery and traditionally styled furnishings, like the country French-style armoires, complete the picture. □

Far left: *A cheery color scheme of yellow, blue, and green imbue this bedroom with impressionistic style. The love seat's fabric is particularly painterly— dashes of color are combined in a Monet-like manner. Furnishings with traditional lines add to the room's romance, but crisp white linens and graphic quilts keep the mood light.*
Left: *Fanciful pillows are creative patchworks of antique linens.*

Upholstery, side table, and armoires by Pennsylvania House. Print fabric by Waverly

A Bittersweet Affair

By Karol K. DeWulf
Produced by
Mary Anne Thomson

John Houser has an eye for the old ladies. He loves to find once stately homes past their prime and restore them to a youthful charm and beauty. Drawing upon diverse artistic talents and experiences, the Spanish teacher and interior designer revives a home's exterior while renewing the interiors with family antiques and traditional detailing.

Although John's affairs with grand old houses have always ended happily, there's a bittersweet twist to his romances. As John enrobes a reclaimed belle in a final coat of paint and bejewels her last room with a handcrafted

Above: John and Anne Houser, along with son Chip and daughter Fran, on their front porch. Eldest daughter Lisa is away at school. Left: The Houser living room is a picture of countrified elegance. Right: A rambling porch graces the exterior of the home.

Photographs: Maris/Semel. Field editor: Eileen A. Deymier

25

John's quest for perfection isn't teamed with the need to live with it. "It's the [process] that's more interesting than the finished project," he says.

chandelier, he feels restless longing rather than content.

"It bothers me when the house is pretty well finished because then I get bored," John says. "And that's when we sell and start all over again."

Fortunately, John is blessed with a family that's supportive of his insatiable appetite for renovating old houses. The Housers have moved eight times in the past 20 years, but, his wife, Anne, maintains an open mind about changing addresses.

"I don't mind [moving]. I enjoy it—I really do," she says lightly. "The houses are an outlet for John's creativity."

John's latest love, an early 1900s home, is nestled among the tall, flowering trees of Kirkwood, Missouri. Although it's now the beauty on the block, the home lacked any distinct style when the family moved in.

"The house is an example of what I call cornball architecture," says John. "You know, a little bit of everything thrown in together."

To distinguish the home's exterior, simple cosmetics were applied.

"Anything to help the old lady out," John muses.

A crisp color contrast now emphasizes the horizontal lines of the home's wraparound porch. A dark red defines the first floor, including a family

Left: A colonial-style floral-print fabric ties together the rich colors of the living room.
Above: The entry is defined by a stenciled "rug" that John fashioned.
Right: Antique decoys the Housers have collected nest in the living room corner cupboard alongside new versions modeled by John.

A Bittersweet Affair

An earlier Houser home is depicted in the fireboard painting. "It's a fun way for us to remember our stone house in the country," John says.

room addition, while the second floor of the house is stucco dressed in a coat of creamy white.

Inside the house, John's make-over magic was considerably more involved. The living room, which had the redeeming qualities of a fireplace and French doors, was a first priority. "We wanted the living room to be dark, inviting, and comfortable," says John. "A room you'd enjoy by candlelight."

To give the room a

decidedly colonial twist, John paneled the fireplace wall with wide tongue-and-groove boards, arched the fireplace opening, and crowned the opening with a vintage mantel.

A sweep of olive green is the wall's—and the room's—finishing touch.

"I'm partial to country painted furniture in blacks, reds, and creams," John explains, "and the [olive] color is a wonderful background for them."

The same palette is

carried throughout the first floor. In the dining room, the colors appear in a "rug" John has stenciled on the floor.

A stenciler before the craft was popularized, John adapts historical motifs from New England for his patterns. He prefers stenciled designs to have an aged look but thinks that it's more a result of time than technique.

"... when we move I hate to leave the floors," he says. "They're just

Opposite: A colonial-styled stenciled "rug" anchors the scrub-top dining table and Hitchcock-style antique chairs.
Above: An antique mantel and a fireboard painting create a focal point in the dining room.
Right: Color drama is added with a hanging Pennsylvania hooked rug.

A Bittersweet Affair

Friend Bill Kelly handcrafted the tin light fixtures that grace the Housers' home. "I stenciled his upstairs in return for a chandelier," says John.

beginning to wear a bit."

The dining room also boasts a painting by John. Applied directly to the plaster wall, the work imitates a fireboard within the framework of the room's antique mantel.

"There are two buildings in the painting: a stone house that we renovated in 1976 and our neighbor's house, which was stone but I painted in brick," says John. "It's a fun way for us to remember our stone house in the country."

Enriching every Houser home, including their present one, are antiques and collectibles that John and Anne have found on numerous trips to Ohio and New England. In addition to providing many treasures and a great deal of pleasure, the antique-hunting trips have seasoned the couple's tastes.

"I try to avoid things with a high shine," says John. "I really like things that have the old finish on them . . . like the old red or black paint finish on most of these furnishings. I like the dull finishes, which I think is a part of the country look."

The Housers' respect for antique furniture is coupled with a high appreciation for craftsmanship and the artisan responsible for it. This regard is perhaps best exemplified by John's admiration of samplers.

"I love samplers because they're a very personal thing," he explains. "A sampler usually is dated and signed by the person who did it. You can find out where it was done and gather a lot of specific information about the piece itself; it seems more historic . . . more real."

Right: *The family room's look of antiquity belies its new construction. The beams were recycled from a 100-year-old St. Louis warehouse.* Above: *Old and new meld in the kitchen. Laminate countertops and modern appliances coexist with a tin chandelier, a pine floor, and country collectibles.*

A Bittersweet Affair

Unlike the samplers he admires, John's handiwork can't be captured in a frame, but it is just as telling of his personal talents and traits. The Houser home reveals stenciling as John's signature; the tenor of fine antiques, his voice; and the promise of renewing a vintage house, his constant inspiration.

The lucky lady has been the object of John's devotion for 4½ years. True to form, John grows restless as he applies the finishing touches. A bittersweet affair coming to a close? Perhaps. But there's always another love for John Houser just around the corner.□

Above: *The dark coziness of the downstairs living areas gives way to light airiness in the upstairs master bedroom, which glows in a garden variety of pinks and peaches.*

April

Country Home.

On the Streets of Philadelphia
Artistry in Home & Craft
The House that Jack (and Judy) Built

On The Streets of Philadelphia

By Ellen Kaye and Linda Joan Smith

Sharp as a pitchfork, soft as a crib quilt, Anne Sims' Philadelphia home is a pleasing study in contrasts. Each room displays an unmistakably personal style based on an artful mix of items, from primitive farm tools to modern art. The feeling is timeless, yet beyond the walls a 20th-century city surges on.

Anne's tiny rooms are full, yet there is no cloying sense of clutter. Instead, her ability to create dynamic compositions—still lifes designed more to amuse than impress—makes her tiny rooms vibrate with vitality. Each stairway landing, each awkward little corridor is transformed by a grouping of collected objects: old, new, and in-between.

"I put things together and see how it works," Anne says. "And if it doesn't work I just try again."

Her ancestry may account in part for Anne's artistic nature; her grandfather was a well-known Philadelphia architect and lithographer. Whether inborn or acquired, her design sense has been honed by her own career in the decorative arts. She has worked for several local museums and is currently an associate of Sotheby's and president

— ■ —

Top: *Framed by leafy greenery, Anne Sims relaxes in her city garden.* Opposite: *Touches of new among the old distinguish Anne's version of the country look. A Jasper Johns flag print flies above a mantel-top display of old wooden spools and pottery.* Left: *Anne freely mixes design eras and styles. Here, a 1925 poster celebrating British industry tops a Pennsylvania blanket chest of the early 1800s.*

Photographs: Tommy Miyasaki, De Gennaro Associates

of the Philadelphia Textile Society.

Anne's home in the city is actually two back-to-back trinities, tiny houses with one room on each of three floors. She rents the composite dwelling from owner John Burris, an architect who says he renovated the adjoining structures as "a fun project, done on a shoestring."

In decorating her home, Anne echoed the atmosphere of the surrounding neighborhood, which is a lively mix of new and old. She resides in the Northern Liberties section of Philadelphia, where young professionals live side by side with descendants of the original middle-Europeans who settled the area in the late 18th century.

Anne moved to the neighborhood in 1981 and began collecting about the same time. Her first infatuations were with quilts, hooked rugs, and rag rugs, which she cherishes for their color, their pattern, and the craft involved in their making. From textiles (still a great love), she progressed to collecting kitchenware, tools, and pottery, and eventually to a miscellany of objects and furniture chosen solely for their visual appeal.

Top: *A sense of serenity, born of Anne's careful compositions, arises from the clutter in the small rooms.* Above: *Anne's passion for old tools, from augers and clamps to handsaws and hayforks, is evident in her dining room, where a workshop's worth fills her walls.* Right: *Anne decorated her kitchen with utilitarian collectibles: graniteware, cooking utensils, breadboards. A drafting table that belonged to her architect grandfather is a cherished piece used for both dining and working.*

HEART OF THE CITY

Anne displays a special passion for old tools, which she collects more for their sculptural quality than for their value as antiques. "I like the idea that they were used," she says. "Even if I don't always know what they were used for."

One of her favorite nontool finds is the colorful penny rug that hangs on the wall in her stairwell. "I bought it for five dollars," she says. "The seller didn't know what it was and neither did I. But I loved its geometric quality."

For Anne, liking a piece—provided it's affordable—is the guiding criterion. "Less-than-perfect pieces of early furniture are still within reach," she says, pointing out a handsome Pennsylvania blanket chest in her living room which dates from the early 1800s. "The legs aren't original and it's been patched in places. The piece has problems, but I still really like it."

Then her museum education takes over, if only for a moment. "That's not the way to collect, really," she says. "The right way is to buy the very best you can afford. But I tend to buy more from the heart, and I don't think I'll ever change." □

Top: *Anne's love of textiles and geometric forms is perfectly expressed by the dramatic penny rug that dominates the stairwell.* Above: *More geometrics dance in the earthy quilts she displays in her bedroom. The trio of lithographs are the work of her grandfather.* Right: *A one-dimensional goose decoy presides over the study, which is warmed by one of the houses' six fireplaces. Surrounding the fireplace is an arrangement of objects designed to amuse: snowshoes, ice skates, and bulbous stoneware jugs.*

ARTISTRY
In Home & Craft

By Estelle Bond Guralnick and Pamela Wilson

For Carroll and Claudia Hopf, marriage is a partnership in more ways than one. Not only do they work together with their son, Perry, as artists—Claudia creates detailed *scherenschnitte* designs, Perry does the paper cuttings, and Carroll is an accomplished grain painter—they recently teamed their talents in the rescue and restoration of a run-down 1800s house.

After suffering years of neglect and a close brush with the wrecking ball, the little house in York County, Maine, finally met with good fortune. Indeed, had the Hopfs not come along, the early 19th-century dwelling might well have been sold to builders who were smitten, not with the house, but the lovely land on which it sat.

As serendipity would have it, the Hopfs (who had been fruitlessly searching for just the right place to accommodate their family-run crafts business) just happened upon the house. They were living in Massachusetts at the time and decided to drive to Maine to entertain a visiting friend. After stopping for lunch, the Hopfs could not resist dropping into a local

Above (bottom): *Claudia, Carroll, and Perry Hopf in front of their restored Maine home.* Left: *A folk art penguin, likely a late-19th- or early 20th-century outdoor advertising piece, greets guests.* Above (top): *Titled "House Blessing," this cut-paper scene and the frame are samples of the Hopfs' work.*

Photographs: William N. Hopkins, Hopkins Associates

Left: *The keeping room features blue-painted woodwork, a red-painted floor, and a newly installed old-fashioned stove. A trio of unmatched banister-back chairs surround the table, which is set 18th-century style with candles at all four corners. Below: An early New England cupboard, with much of its original red finish still showing, displays a collection of English ceramics and German steins, all from the 18th century. Above: A pair of hollow-cut silhouettes from Claudia's collection adorns one keeping-room wall.*

real estate office and presenting the agent with a list of their wants: specifically, an antique fixer-upper with a center chimney, a pretty staircase, nice little front hall, and a barn that could be converted into a crafts studio.

Whereas other agents had been stumped by the couple's requirements, this one was not. Claudia recalls the agent saying, "Can you wait fifteen minutes? I think I have just the house for you."

As luck would have it, explains Claudia, "The agent was showing the house to some other people who walked in the front door and out the back as fast as they could."

The Hopfs' reaction was decidedly different. Instead of fleeing from the run-down dwelling and debris-filled barn, they lingered. Overlooking the crumbling plaster, exposed lath, crayon-marked walls, decal-covered windows, and mice-infested barn, they saw wonderful potential in the sad but basically sound structures. Says Claudia of that day in March 1985, "I had the place furnished in my mind's eye before we left." By the next week, they were negotiating to buy the house, and the sale went through in May.

According to research completed by the Hopfs, the history of their house dates back to 1822, when it was owned by Rufus Furbush, a blacksmith. They speculate that the earliest part of the structure might have been moved from another site and perhaps dates to 1800. In

1830, the dining room and kitchen were added, and the barn went up about 10 years later. Earlier in this century, the home was owned by a horticulturist who planted wonderful gardens on the 1¾-acre lot. "People would take strolls just to admire the gardens," says Claudia.

Home & Craft

Right: *Furnished austerely with straight-back chairs, the Hopfs' front parlor speaks of an era when excess comfort was frowned upon.* Below: *The less-formal dining room features blue-green woodwork outlined with a wallpaper border—a treatment typical of the Federal period.* Above: *These contemporary hand-carved and -painted snakes are just-for-fun folk art in the Hopfs' dining room.*

Unfortunately, the property fell on hard times after the death of that homeowner and the subsequent deaths of his wife and a housekeeper. For a period of seven years it was used as a rental. "The house was unloved, and it reflected it," says Claudia. It was a far cry from the showplace that strollers came to admire.

Determined to restore its original character, the first thing the Hopfs did to the house was replace the two-over-two windows with nine-over-sixes and paint the exterior a warm gold. "That's when the neighbors started saying hello," says Claudia.

The next step was the interior—a case of starting from scratch. New plumbing was installed, and the electrical system was extended. As a matter of survival and maintaining sanity, the Hopfs worked on one room at a time, making sure that the front parlor was completed before they moved in, "to remind us of home," says Claudia. They furnished the room with three chairs, a table, and a changing display of bouquets. "It was an oasis for us."

It wasn't until August—after they finally installed a bathroom—that the three Hopfs were able to move in. After all, the house was far from habitable when the papers were signed, and it had taken an entire summer of juggling their business in Massachusetts and work on the house in Maine just to ready the place for "camping out" occupancy.

One of the most demanding projects was lifting latter-day flooring to reveal old, wide floorboards. In the kitchen, Carroll thought he was finished when he got to the second layer of flooring. But no, the prying of a crowbar revealed five more layers, including newspapers from the

Left: *Folk art abounds in the Hopfs' master bedroom, as do many fine examples of early painted finishes.*
Below: *This picture-perfect corner vignette features curtains by Claudia, a mid-1800s hanging shelf, assorted band boxes, and a delightful doll with hair made of bearskin.*
Above: *An early sewing box has fanciful folk-art bird carvings, a pincushion, and spindles for thread.*

1800s, layers of linoleum, even a newish wood floor.

When necessary, the Hopfs employed a professional plasterer and carpenter; otherwise, they completed the work themselves. For example, when the dining room and keeping room ceilings needed to be replastered, they called in a professional. But to give the rooms the unevenly textured, aged effect that the house demanded, Perry finished the ceilings with a coating of joint compound applied with a trowel. They also transformed the main floor of the barn into a studio for their crafts business and the loft into living quarters for Perry.

Upon completing the restoration work, the Hopfs turned their talents to decoration, producing delightful results. Each room in the house is a treasure trove of antiques, contemporary folk art, and both old and new traditional crafts.

Philosophically, the family likes to live with old things. They are admirers of fine craftsmanship and are intrigued with the history of old furnishings and collectibles. But their fascination with antiques doesn't exclude the work of contemporary craftspeople. As Claudia points out, "Just because something is old doesn't mean that it's good."

What the Hopfs seek are the best examples of both past and present. They discriminate, not on the basis of age, but on craftsmanship, design, and color: "Those good designs that last forever and can be enjoyed in any age," Claudia explains. "What we do in our house is show how old and new mix, so that visitors can see how well they blend."

Carroll, who is both artist and historian, is particularly interested in painted finishes, viewing them as a type of social document. "Painted

Right: *Overnight guests are invariably enchanted with their stencil-embellished sleeping quarters. Claudia did the work herself, taking inspiration from 19th-century stencil artist Moses Eaton.*
Below: *Decorated Hopf-style with silhouettes, a black-bear sculpture carved from a tree root, and an old Hessian soldier whirligig, the upstairs hall is a standout.*
Above: *A contemporary wood sculpture depicting Adam and Eve in the Garden of Eden.*

furniture has always talked to us," he says. "Most painted furniture was utilitarian but reflected a will in people to embellish their lives with color. Years ago, we lived in a wood-oriented society. There was so much wood it engendered an urge to add color. So people whitewashed walls, painted floors, added color to conceal wood." Furniture, explains Carroll, was a perfect thing to paint, a practice probably harking back to an early peasant tradition from central Europe.

It's obvious that this appreciation of an early life-style has not only found a place in the Hopfs' hearts but in their home.

"What we've concentrated on through the years is the saving of old finishes," says Claudia of the many pieces they use daily. When the couple first started collecting 25 years ago—for Carroll it was even earlier, when he was in high school—it was common for people to destroy old milk-paint finishes by refinishing furniture. "Luckily, that kind of thinking has changed."

Other remnants of the past that find a place in the Hopf home include old textiles that Claudia has collected since the days they were considered rags by others. She first became interested in them while Carroll was enrolled in the museum studies program sponsored by State University of New York at the New York State Historical Association in Cooperstown.

"I saw that the common man used textiles to soften rooms and enrich lives," she explains. They also make vivid the lives of 18th- and 19th-century women and children, she says, citing the loving stitches that went into samplers done by children. Indeed, for each of the Hopfs, connecting with the past is what antique collecting is all about.

Left: *Perry's suite was an open barn loft when the Hopfs bought their home. During the renovation, the floors were leveled, insulation added, and partitions installed to divide the space and accommodate a bathroom.*
Below: *Perry describes his room as a "typical New England setting" complete with period pieces and folk art he has collected.*
Above: *An English knife and fork set with beaded handles is a rare find, according to the Hopfs, who date it to 1680 from the Charles II period.*

Appropriately, Claudia has made all the curtains in the house (and did the stenciling, too), using an 18th-century style called "festoon curtains." As intended by homemakers until at least the mid-19th century, her bed and window treatments are designed to be both functional and decorative—adding warmth, color, and design to rooms.

Although Claudia's first love is creating *scherenschnitte*, she has numerous other passions as well. One of her favorite pastimes is collecting hollow-cut silhouettes, shadow representations of common folk who lived in 18th-century Europe and America. "Just as we exchange snapshots, people in those days would exchange silhouettes," she explains. Numerous examples of these shadow cuttings grace the house, often offering design inspiration for her own work.

The three Hopfs all like to collect "make-do" household items that have been uniquely repaired in earlier times to extend their usability. Today, such pieces help document the actual day-to-day existence of the people who used them. "We hear a lot about the early aristocracy, but it's the pieces used commonly in everyday living that reveal our history," says Carroll.

Using the ways of the past as their guide to the present, the Hopfs' world is a melding of antiques and traditional crafts. They eat from pewterware that friends have made. They sleep in handcrafted beds, now antiques, warmed by quilts stitched generations ago. And they earn their livelihood using the time-honored

traditions of craftspeople before them. "We want to foster the idea of traditional crafts," says Carroll, "so we live by it." □

BUILDING THE COUNTRY HOUSE

The House that Jack (and Judy) Built

By John Riha
Produced by Ruth Reiter

On a wide wooded lot in a quiet suburb of Atlanta sits the dream-come-true house of Jack and Judy Hamilton. It is a storybook home with simple, graceful lines, inviting porches, and comfortable colors. It was built with pride and affection, and the account of its construction is a tale with a happy ending. Thoroughly researched ideas and years of careful planning made building this house a smooth and uncomplicated process.

"We started thinking about this home ten years ago," says Judy, an interior designer. "We knew that when our three boys started growing up we'd all need more space and a sense of privacy. We would have loved to restore an older home, but we just couldn't find what we wanted in the style and the floor plans of the antebellum homes in the Atlanta area. We were after something that had a

Above: *Homeowners Jack and Judy Hamilton of Atlanta wanted a farmhouse look for their newly built home. A simple facade belies the generous amounts of interior space.* Opposite: *A wide deck with outdoor wicker furniture and a gazebo-enclosed whirlpool tub provide a relaxing outdoor area.*

Photographs: Rick Taylor

53

UPPER LEVEL

MAIN LEVEL

farmhouse look to it yet included modern conveniences and plenty of space."

Research became the heart and soul of the Hamiltons' building plan. Drives to the country to look at farmhouses revealed shapes and designs that Jack and Judy found especially pleasing. They also clipped and filed magazine photographs showing architectural details that they liked. Because the Hamiltons had collected antique furniture for years, they were able to envision special places for some of their favorite pieces.

Left: *Hardboard siding and wood ceiling boards with a beaded detailing give a turn-of-the-century appearance to the front porch.* Top: *An antique rocking horse and an 1850s bench from Pennsylvania greet visitors at the entry.* Above: *Plenty of wide open spaces are the heart and soul of the Hamiltons' plans.*

Illustration: Carson Ode

BUILDING THE COUNTRY HOUSE

"What helped most of all were the pictures from the magazines," says Judy. "That way, I was able to show our builder exactly what we had in mind."

After years of planning, it was time for the Hamiltons to turn their visions into reality. Their boys had all grown into teenagers, and their need for bigger space was a pressing concern. When some land came up for sale in a nearby neighborhood, the Hamiltons bought a lot and began to put all their ideas down on paper. They took their sketches to a plan-drawing service to obtain working blueprints, and by June of 1985 they were ready to build the house of their dreams.

The Hamiltons credit much of their project's success to an excellent local builder, George Bramlett.

"We were fortunate to have George as our builder," says Jack. "He was very patient, even though he was building a

Left: *"The family room is our favorite room," says Jack. Hand-hewn beams accent the tall vaulted ceiling. The mantel was cut from an old black-walnut beam.* Top: *An antique Mennonite table is at the center of the family eating area.* Above: *A wide-open kitchen provides easy access to the family room.*

lot of things he hadn't built before. Everything we wanted to do he figured out a way to do it. He made it easy, and I'd have to say that I enjoyed the building process."

Several major features became central to the Hamiltons' plans. A gabled upper level with symmetrically placed dormer windows gives the appearance of a small 1½-story farmhouse. But appearances can be deceiving: the upper level actually contains four

bedrooms and two baths. With Jack and Judy's master bedroom on the first floor, the Hamiltons' three sons have plenty of space—and privacy—on the upper level. A keeping room with a vaulted ceiling adds a spacious touch to the main level.

Outside, a 12-foot-wide deck at the back of the house gives plenty of room for outdoor living in Georgia's temperate climate. Judy designed an exquisite railing that was produced by a local

Left: *Judy's flair for interior design is evident in the living room. Red-and-white reproduction wing chairs and antique quilts mix with the contemporary sofas.* Top: *Generous windows light the living area. The blanket chest is from Judy's parents.* Above: *An antique table from Kentucky highlights the dining room.*

millwork shop under Bramlett's direction. Gingerbread trim was selected from a catalog. The deck features a gazebo that camouflages a large whirlpool tub.

"The house was designed to create a good flow," says Judy. "The living room, sun-room, family room, and deck all work together."

Jack adds, "We have the dream house that we talked about for years." □

Above: *Judy likes "the mood changes" of the house, and the Hamiltons both enjoy the soft tones of the master bedroom. The front-facing windows have solid shutters for privacy and light control.* Left: *Although it's shaded by trees in the summer, this cozy sun-room is filled with light during winter.*

June

Country Home

The Cottage on Daisy Hill
Humble Heart

The COTTAGE On DAISY HILL

By John Riha

Bill and Nancy Boettger built a log house from a kit and created a wonderfully romantic country home.

One day in 1982, Bill and Nancy Boettger followed a road detour, got lost, and found a dream. Driving through the countryside near their Pennsylvania home, the Boettgers took a wrong turn and discovered a small country store nestled on a grassy lot at a quiet back-roads intersection. When they learned that the property was for sale, Bill and Nancy were thrilled. The Boettgers had been looking for something to do on their own, and the idea of restoring and running a country store appealed to their independent natures. They purchased the property and some

Opposite: *The style of Bill and Nancy Boettger's new home was influenced by French-Canadian and European cottage architecture.*
Below: *Bill and Nancy greet visitors to their country store.*

Photographs: Bill Stites

additional acreage and began planning their future.

"So here we were with this nice acreage," says Bill, "and our next thought was, 'Let's build a house on it.' Of course, having lived in old stone houses and other unusual homes for a while, it was obvious that we wouldn't build some contemporary, routine sort of house. We wanted interesting architecture."

Intrigued with the idea of building a home from a package, the Boettgers began to explore the marketplace for kit homes. The more they looked, the more they became attracted to the idea of a log home.

"I was pushing for a log home all along," says Nancy, "because so much of modern construction is so high-tech. I wanted to go back to simpler, older methods of building."

Although many kit log homes were available, the Boettgers became disappointed with the similarity of the home designs. Character became the key word in the search for their own residence. Then a magazine advertisement for a Canadian manufacturer of log homes caught Bill's eye.

"The picture in the advertisement jumped out of the page," says Bill. "It showed a house with a high-pitched, curved-metal roof and dormers. It was close to Nancy's idea of a cottage, which is what she was hoping for. It was great."

As soon as they could, the Boettgers traveled to Quebec to visit the log home manufacturer and examine

Right: *An open floor plan creates a light-filled living room in the Boettgers' home. Structural beams take the place of load-bearing partition walls.* Below: *The Boettgers took one of the kit home manufacturer's basic designs and added custom modifications.*

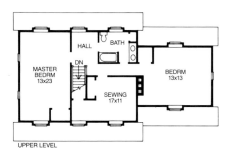

UPPER LEVEL

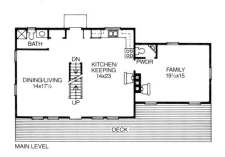

MAIN LEVEL

some of the homes the company had built in the area. What they found were sturdy homes with designs heavily influenced by French-Canadian and European traditions. The construction method employed square-cut logs with tight-fitting joints that all but camouflaged the fact that the structures were actually made of logs.

"We came away convinced that this company, Patriot Log Homes, had a very good product," says Bill. "We felt they were good people and that they would back you up. The log package was super. But I have to stress that the reason we selected it was because it was so architecturally interesting."

Bill and Nancy chose a 1½-story kit with four dormer windows in the upper level and a centrally placed chimney. A few custom modifications of their own design gave the Boettgers approximately 2,000 square feet of living space. Heavy timbers supporting the second story preempted the need for structural partition walls and allowed an open floor plan at the entry level. The steeply pitched roof ensured that the upper level had 8-foot-high ceilings and plenty of space.

Left: *Compact convenience is the theme of the kitchen, with a custom countertop and backsplash of solid cherry wood adding a warming glow. The yellow pine strip flooring is part of the log home kit.* Below: *Nancy's sewing room hints at the generous spaces found on the second level.*

BUILDING THE COUNTRY HOUSE

"The roof is such a strong feature that it could almost look top-heavy from outside," says Nancy. "So we extended the porch deck and added wide front steps to help anchor the house."

The distinctive red curved-metal roof is supported by truss framing and enhances the European-influenced design the Boettgers found so attractive. Nancy's enthusiasm for cottage architecture also led her to add special details that give the house its character. Decorative crosses appear at the apex of the gable ends of the roof as well as in the dormers, and rows of fishscale shingles cover the space between the log structure and the brick foundation. The crowning touch is found at the uppermost part of the house, where clay chimney pots reach into the sky.

In 29 years of marriage Bill and Nancy have lived in a variety of fine homes, including an 18th-century stone house. But their kit log home represents the ultimate in satisfaction.

"When all is said and done," says Bill, "what we have is an expression of how we want to live." □

Right: *Despite outward appearances, the upper level of the Boettgers' home is characterized by high ceilings and generous amounts of space. In the master bedroom, dormer windows admit plenty of light.* Below: *A cozy upstairs guest bedroom reflects European charm.*

HUMBLE HEART

By Deborah Hufford and John Riha
Produced by Mary Anne Thomson

I knew by the smoke,
 that so gracefully curl'd
Above the green elms,
 that a cottage was near,
And I said, "If there's peace
 to be found in the world,
A heart that was humble
 might hope for it here!"

—Thomas Moore, 1804

Photographs: William N. Hopkins, Hopkins Associates

HUMBLE HEART

Below: *Susie Van Sickle enjoys living with history and nature in an 1800s pioneer cabin in a valley near Hermann, Missouri.*
Opposite: *Originally a dogtrot between two cabins, the entryway was enclosed in 1904 to combine the structures.*
Left: *The porches overlook landscaped gardens of herbs and flowers and the beautiful valley beyond.*

In the morning it is cool. Sunlight brushes the tops of the gentle Missouri hills, but shrouds of mist still linger in the shadowed fields, caressing the grasses with sparkling dew. From where she sits on her front porch, Susie Van Sickle can see miles of rolling landscape stretched out in quiet contentment. Behind her house, where the maples, oaks, and dogwoods crowd close, the whippoorwills jump and sing and cry, heralding the end of another summer's night.

"I just love to listen to the animals," says Susie, sipping on a mug of fresh tea. "The whippoorwills out here are wonderful— they wake you up in the morning. If you're not used to them, they could drive you crazy. But I love it! You can come out here and smell the country and eat your herbs. We have a lot of bluebirds, and the hummingbirds love the comfrey. It's just really rewarding to me."

Susie first came to the countryside around Hermann, Missouri, more than six years ago. She was living in Jefferson City and making pilgrimages to the Hermann area to look for antiques. Enchanted with the beauty of the Missouri River Valley, Susie became determined to move there. Her search for a place to live was a quest for a new and peaceful way of life.

"I knew what I was looking for," says Susie. "I wanted something that was old, something that could be restored, something that wasn't modernized. I must have looked at forty structures before making a decision."

The place that captured Susie's heart was indeed anything but modern. Originally built as a French trapper's log cabin in the 1820s, long before Hermann was settled, the humble house sat tucked up against the broad hills. German pioneers of the 1840s had added a stone

Opposite: *Log and mortar walls and primitive antiques create the spirit of the wilderness in the cabin's living room.*
Left: *An 1830s blue chestnut cupboard from Virginia is flanked by hickory-woven chairs once used in Susie's grandparents' Minnesota cabin.*
Below: *A 1735 lift-top blanket box shares a comely corner with a Rhode Island sampler. Aromatic herbs hang in each room.*

addition and more recent owners had repaired the old foundation and the stone exterior, but for the most part the old homestead was badly in need of work. The walls were unfinished, there were no cupboards or trim, windowsills were rotting, and there were gaping holes in the floorboards. But Susie loved it.

"Once I found this old place I just knew this was what I wanted," recalls Susie. "When I walked in the door I got as far as the entry and said, *This is it! I don't want to leave without this house.*"

Susie purchased the old house and with it 125 rolling acres. Moving to the area with her daughter, Jeralyn, Susie opened an antiques shop in Hermann and dug in her heels for the long months of work ahead.

Susie remembers the trial of the first few chilly winters when not all of the rooms had sources of heat. "You did get cold, and you

HUMBLE HEART

Opposite: *An airy dining room is drenched in morning sun while Tasha, the family's golden retriever, lazes under a pine table.*
Left: *A hand-thrown crock awaits a bouquet of wild daisies beneath a reproduction fixture by St. Louis tinsmith Carl Ritchie. The dining room window affords a magnificent view of the valley.*
Below: *The renovated kitchen provides an efficient but pleasant center for Susie's ambitious herbal cooking projects.*

did scurry to the bath where there was a space heater," says Susie, "but surprisingly you get used to it. As long as you were doing something you were fine. It's when I sat down to watch TV or write a letter that my teeth would chatter. I know I complained, but I don't look back on it as being horrible. As we got heat into the log room we'd block the rest of it off with blankets and sheets."

The first order of business for Susie was to take care of the essentials. Holes in the flooring were fixed and a new plumbing system installed. "We were fortunate," says Susie. "The house hadn't been modernized, so there wasn't a lot to tear out."

Susie then had new electrical and heating systems put in and replaced old windows with new insulating glass

windows. The master bedroom's original stone fireplace had been completely blocked up and was restored to working condition.

Susie's long-term goal was to maintain the cabin's primal spirit. Much of the natural textures in the home were retained. In the keeping room, for example, exposed hand-hewn beams and rough log-and-mortar walls preserve the handsome rustic character inherent in the structure.

Once the old house was again structurally sound and livable, Susie set about furnishing and decorating the interiors. Although Susie sought to remain faithful to the original spirit of the house, she also desired all the modern conveniences. "I wanted a great look but everything at my fingertips," she says.

HUMBLE
HEART

Right *and* far right: *The
master bedroom is part
of the original 1840s
stone cabin. Stenciling
on a portion of the floor
is a continuation of the
original pattern. The
limestone fireplace had
to be restored to
working condition.*
Below: *Fragrant rubrum
lilies from Susie's
gardens accent the
wide windowsill.*

To help her with the
interiors, Susie enlisted
the talents of her friend
Bruce Berstert, a Kansas
City decorator. "Bruce had
an excellent eye for
balance and proportion,"
Susie says.

Moving methodically
from room to room, Bruce
and Susie created looks
that gave each space an air
of authenticity. To create
the look of old plaster,
Bruce stippled the walls in
the master bedroom and
kitchen. In the second-
level family room and in
Jeralyn's bedroom, old
roof sheathing boards and
pole rafters were left in
place to take advantage of
their rustic beauty. A new
roof and shingles were
applied over the old
framing members to
ensure that the once-leaky
structure would shed the
hardest rains.

"Bruce and I went
through a lot of ideas in
the family room," says
Susie. "The room was very
dark, and I didn't want it
to be that way. I wanted as
much storage as possible
because there was no other
storage in the house. We
also wanted to conceal the
TV, stereo, and computer."

HUMBLE HEART

Below: *A bright checkerboard-stenciled floor and whitewashed ceiling open up the upstairs family room. An old green mantel Susie had collected was installed for the fireplace. She chose a matching green for the storage cupboards.*
Right: *Susie's daughter, Jeralyn, lounges with Tasha in her loft bedroom. Susie and Bruce created an airy freshness in the room by hanging shirred fabric on tension rods mounted between the rafters.*

To lighten up the family room, Susie and Bruce whitewashed the original roof sheathing. The mantel was a piece of architectural salvage that Susie found and had cut to fit the fireplace opening. Bruce also designed and painted the large checkerboard floor pattern.

"The family room is really cozy to me. I like to spend time in there, and it doubles as a guest room," Susie says.

"Bruce added so many special touches," Susie notes, and cites the stenciled floor designs which were also strokes of his expertise. "Bruce picked up the leaf pattern which was original to the structure. I sort of knew what I wanted, and he put it together for me," Susie says. The bright floor designs in the family room and keeping room add refreshing touches and still work in well with the rustic interior.

The cabin provides a homey setting for Susie's extensive collection of primitive antiques, especially pre-Civil War furniture.

"I like to use things from local craftspeople," Susie says, and points out the many textiles, locally handcrafted pottery, and the back porch twig furniture made by an Arkansas artisan.

The porch is also decorated with a profusion of potted flowers and dried spices from Susie's gardens. It is here that she enjoys morning tea, entertains guests on summer evenings, or just takes in the scenery.

"I sit in a beautiful valley, and not too many people that come here don't love it," says Susie. "There are a lot of people who don't understand this life-style. But I like the peacefulness." □

August

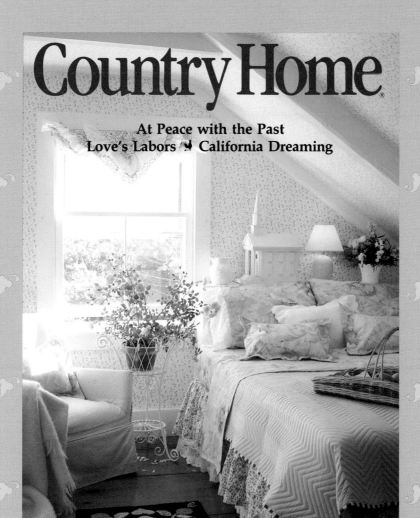

Country Home

At Peace with the Past
Love's Labors ❧ California Dreaming

At Peace · with · the · Past

Above: *Dennis and Will Bellar bought this proud 1830s stone house in St. Charles, Missouri—twice.*
Opposite: *The inviting entry was originally a dogtrot porch between the main house and its summer kitchen. Now enclosed, its stone wall is the perfect backdrop for an 1850s deacon's bench.*
Right: *Dennis shows off part of her collection of soft-paste Dutch dishes.*

"My husband says it's like Grandma's house,"
says Dennis Bellar.
"Everybody loves to
come here because it's
big and comfortable."

By John Riha

Photographs: William N. Hopkins, Hopkins Associates. Field editor: Mary Anne Thomson

82

"Love is wonderful," the song goes, "the second time around." Just ask Dennis Bellar and her husband, Will. They've fallen in love with their 1830s house—twice.

"We bought this house the first time in 1975," says Dennis, "and we lived there until 1976. But we decided that there was too much to be done to it. Our daughter was an infant at the time and it was hard to have a brand-new baby and have to work on the house, too. So we moved to Chesterfield in St. Louis and lived there for six years. But we missed this house. We really wanted it back. We called the owners and it took them about two years to make up their minds to sell it back to us, and we're glad they did."

The object of this twice-told tale is a two-story house of quarried stone located in St. Charles County, Missouri. It was built in the 1830s by Scottish immigrant James Lindsey on a 3,500-acre land grant. Although Lindsey's original floor plan has been altered by various remodeling projects, the structure's proud, unadorned facade is a testament to the patience and building skill of Missouri's early settlers.

"St. Charles has the biggest concentration of early Missouri homes in the state," says Dennis. "People who visit here just can't say enough about how they love the atmosphere and the old buildings."

In the Bellars' home, care has been taken to get the maximum amount of usage from the available space. An entryway separating the main house from a summer kitchen was enclosed and passage doors eliminated so that the summer kitchen, family room, and entryway merge. The old summer kitchen now includes the Bellars' kitchen and dining areas and creates an area that is perfect for entertaining. The Bellars also contained the family living area and bedrooms to the main level of the house, creating guest rooms in the upper level. The arrangement offers convenient privacy for the Bellars' many out-of-town visitors.

"The man who we originally bought the house from, Don Mosley, had done the major restoration work," says Will. "We added some special touches, like putting stone

Opposite: *The family room is filled with lighthearted and casual furnishings. An old window well was converted to a built-in display cabinet.*
Above: *In the family room a cherished 18th-century corner cupboard shows off a collection of antique toys.*
Left: *A long walnut dining table can serve 12 guests in the converted summer kitchen.*

flooring at the entry and installing pine boards in the den that match the house's original flooring."

One of the best features of Dennis and Will's house, however, is the many fine pieces of antique furniture they have collected over the years. Every corner and wall is home to some unique and interesting treasure that holds special meaning for the Bellars.

"Most of the things we have are things we like to live with and have had for years and years," says Dennis. "I'm not interested in crafts or reproductions, so everything I have is old." The Bellars' fascination with antiques led Dennis to become a dealer, but Dennis prefers to describe herself as a "collector-dealer."

"Everything some dealers buy is for sale," she says. "But, like many dealers, I keep the things that I like for myself." Dennis and Will have lived in their dream house more than six years, and the qualities they enjoy most are virtually indescribable.

"We love this place," says Dennis. "My husband says it's like Grandma's house. Everybody loves to come here because it's big, comfortable, and casual." □

Left: *The second-story bedrooms are devoted to guests. Spacious closets and extra quilts would make any visitor feel right at home.*
Above: *The master bedroom is on the main floor. The chest of drawers is dated 1800.*

Love's Labors

"Renovations can be tiring and frustrating," says Bob Dykes. "But after everything is done, you're glad you stuck it out."

By John Riha

Opposite: *Ray Beckmann and Bob Dykes' elegant Federal-style home was built in downtown St. Charles in the mid-1800s.*
Left: *An 1850s wagon bench and an antique rag rug accent the entry.*
Top: *Ray displays part of his extensive collection of woven baskets made by Swedish immigrant Monroe Johnson in the late 1800s.*

Photographs: William N. Hopkins, Hopkins Associates. Field editor: Mary Anne Thomson

Ray Beckmann may not have followed his grandfather's footsteps as a maker of fine furniture, but the St. Charles, Missouri, homeowner did inherit a keen appreciation for superior craftsmanship and well wrought details. It was an admiration that shaped Ray's life and led him to the 153-year-old brick structure that he now calls home.

"I've always been interested in old things," says Ray. "Many of the houses in St. Charles are old, and if you want to live in one, you have to fix it up."

Born and raised in St. Louis County, Ray traveled often to nearby St. Charles to visit relatives. Members of his family have lived in St. Charles since the 1850s. Not surprisingly, Ray became interested in old furniture, and with his partner, Bob Dykes, eventually set up an antiques shop in the historic district of St. Charles.

"One of the nice things about St. Charles is that it's a country town," says Ray. "It has the rural atmosphere, but you can still see all the cultural events of St. Louis."

Bob began searching for just the right older residence to buy and restore. He had a special feeling for an 1830s Federal-style home that was located just down the street from their antiques store. When the house finally did come up for sale, Bob bought it and set about restoring the home to its original condition.

A stickler for authenticity, Bob made sure that rooms rearranged and altered by previous owners were

Right: *A rocker made by freed Civil War slave William Kunze and a wooden footstool made by Ray's grandfather lend simple elegance to the living room.* Above: *A cherry corner cupboard with glass doors dating to 1844 holds Ray's collection of blue willow dinnerware.*

returned to their 1850 locations. All of the work was supervised to ensure the integrity of the look. Original stenciling, still intact on old plaster walls, was copied and reproduced wherever it was found.

"I did most of the decorating," says Ray. "I'm a perfectionist that way. I like to have my hand on the pulse of things."

Authentic wall colors and meticulous craftsmanship became the backdrop for Ray and Bob's extensive collection of antiques and primitives. An avid collector, Ray specializes in Missouri-made pieces. His collection of chairs made by freed Civil War slave William Kunze is one of the finest in the state.

Ray finds many of his antique

pieces in out-of-the-way places and takes great pleasure in going to antiques shows and auctions in rural areas of Missouri. It was at a farm auction that Ray first discovered the baskets made in the late 1800s by Monroe Johnson, a Swedish immigrant who settled in Missouri. Ray's fascination with Johnson's baskets led him to collect many fine examples and eventually write a book on the subject.

Now a veteran of a major home restoration, Ray could probably write a book on that subject, too.

"We both agree that renovations can be tiring and frustrating," says Ray, "and it seems like you never reach the end. But after everything is done, you're glad you stuck it out."

Right: *A second-story bedroom is dominated by a four-poster maple rope bed. A pine blanket chest is the perfect spot to display a model of the Queen Mary.* Above: *A Missouri-made walnut linen press from 1840 holds an intriguing collection of antique toys.*

California DREAMING

A FAMILY'S LOVE AFFAIR WITH A HOUSE IN THE HILLS

By Barbara Cathcart and Linda Joan Smith

Left: Jack and Joan Simon and their children, Laura, 18, and Brett, 14, live in the hills south of San Francisco. They waited longingly for seven years to buy their house. Far left: This protected brick patio area opens off a glassed-in sun-room. It's a romantic spot for sunny summer breakfasts and alfresco suppers.

Eighteen years have passed since Jack and Joan Simon first heard the quiet voice of this house in the hills, murmuring a domestic song that called them to the pleasures of home. Tucked along a quiet road and sheltered by towering trees, the house seemed meant for them. But for seven long years after their dreams of owning it began, the house was not for sale.

The Simons stumbled across the house soon after they moved to California from New York. Jack, now a psychiatrist, was a resident at a hospital south of San Francisco. After hectic days at the hospital, he and Joan would stroll quietly through the nearby hills. It was on one of those walks that they first noticed the dwelling.

"We fell in love with it," Joan says. "Quite simply, it was our house." Over the next seven years,

Photographs: Tommy Miyasaki, De Gennaro Associates. Interior design: Joan Simon

96

they made a point of arranging their walks to include a pass by the house, never quite giving up their dream.

With Jack's residency complete, he and Joan planned to take a year off and travel across Europe with their children, Laura and Brett. On the eve of their trip, however, a friend called to tell them the house was finally on the market. Without a moment's hesitation the Simons canceled their travel plans. That was 11 years ago.

"We've never regretted that decision for a single moment," Jack says. Finally, in 1977, the Simons moved into their new house. For them, it truly felt like coming home.

Though for years the Simons had

glimpsed the house only from afar, the interior of the house turned out to be just what they had imagined. The only major remodeling work they did was in the kitchen; otherwise, the basic structure of the house remains just as it did when it was built 52 years ago.

What gives the house its special look, however, is not so much the structure as the loving touch Joan, an interior designer, has lavished on each room. Throughout the house she has mixed European furniture and ceramics with American antiques and reproductions for a refreshing country look that springs directly from her singular tastes.

Particularly in evidence are pieces

Left: *Joan mixed comfortable contemporary couches with antiques and reproductions in the living room to give it a gracious, timeless air.*
Right: *A constellation of faience plates brightens the room.*
Above: *Standing tall in a corner of the living room is this miniature French town house, which Joan had made by a San Francisco artist.*

from Joan's collection of faience, European folk pottery with a lengthy history. Joan bought her first pieces on a trip to Portugal nine years ago.

"We hand carried them home on the plane," Joan says. "Both of our children were given ten plates to take care of. They were really very good sports about it."

Her first group of plates has been added to many times since then, as Joan has discovered special pieces —both new and antique—on subsequent trips to France, Portugal, Italy, and Spain. Now the collection, much of which is displayed on the living room wall (shown on the *previous page*), seems to grow by itself. "People know I collect faience and have brought me many pieces," says Joan. "That's nice because I can look around and be reminded of my friends."

A few faience pieces decorate the sun-room, *left*, which is one of Joan's favorite spots in the house. To turn this area into a usable year-round room, the Simons glassed in a portion of an outdoor patio. French doors now connect the room with the garden area beyond, and chintz-covered wicker, both new and old, gives the one-time patio an English air.

"It's a marvelous spot on winter mornings for that extra cup of coffee, sitting in the sunlight," Joan says.

The atmosphere in the nearby

Left: *Sunlight streams into this comfortable sitting area, which was once part of the backyard patio.* Right: *Joan turned the excess space at one end of the living room into a cozy writing nook with a 19th-century English desk.* Above: *A collection of favorite items—glass marbles, an antique letter box, family pictures—bring a personal touch to the desk top.*

dining room, *left,* is imported from Portugal and the South of France, climatic cousins to the Simons' California home. The dining table and chairs have a decidedly French provincial feel, while the needlepoint carpet was ordered on the Simons' first trip to Portugal nine years ago. The carpet didn't arrive until just last year.

Although the dining room was well suited to the Simons' entertaining needs, they longed for a more casual family eating area. The kitchen, *below,* yielded the needed space after a remodeling that opened up the sink wall of the room and did away with a butler's pantry. Joan chose a turn-of-the-century American oak table and

chairs for this comfortable kitchen spot; they add further to the appealing melting-pot mix so evident throughout the house.

It's that freedom to mix and match, says Joan, that's one of the most exciting parts of decorating. Her skill at this artful blending is especially evident in the master bedroom (shown on the *next page*). Again, souvenirs from European trips help create an elegant country feeling.

The delicate pink pillow shams and sheets were unearthed in an antique-linen store in the South of France. The pair of botanical prints on the wall are from London, as is the clock face and the small watercolor. On the floor is

Left: *A Portuguese rug sets the color mood for the dining room; Joan waited patiently for eight years to receive it.* Right: *The Simons remodeled the kitchen to make room for a family dining table.* Above: *Part of Joan's collection of faience pottery.*

another Portuguese needlepoint rug.

"The funny thing is, when the rug for the dining room came, this rug was also in the package," Joan explains. "It had been so long, I'd forgotten I'd ordered it." Amazingly, the colors were exactly right for the bedroom.

Joan arranged a cozy reading nook in one corner of the room, again drawing on a miscellaneous collection of items, from a Victorian sewing table to a clock that was a wedding present.

"I do have a number of collections," Joan admits. "But actually, neither Jack nor I are that attached to them." She pauses, then smiles. "What we are attached to is this house." That attachment shows in every room. □

Above: *Floral prints, soft peach walls, and an English garden bench set a romantic country mood for the master bedroom.*
Left: *Comfort is one of Joan's decorating bywords; she loves to include inviting upholstered pieces.*

October

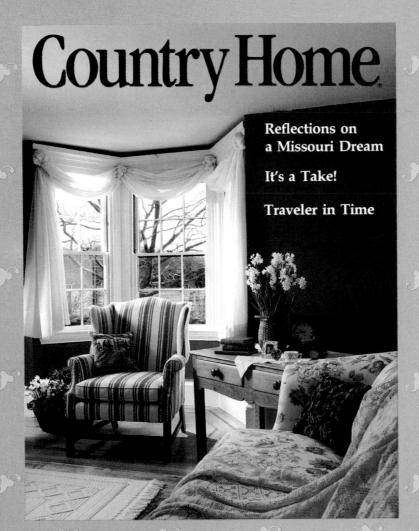

Country Home.

Reflections on
a Missouri Dream

It's a Take!

Traveler in Time

Reflections On A Missouri Dream

Rich and Carolyn Green poured years of labor—and love—into renovating their 120-year-old stone farmhouse.

By John Riha
Produced by Mary Anne Thomson

Dreams can be elusive. Many are nothing more than vapors, easily scattered by the slightest unfavorable winds. But some dreams are vision quests, shining images that are brought to reality only after years of hope and hard work.

Rich and Carolyn Green know well the long-sought dream. When job changes brought the Greens and their two children, Nicole and Scott, *right,* to central Missouri, they longed to find the right house to call their own. Their hopes had been tempered by years of living in a restored log-and-plank home in Illinois, and they expected to discover a similar treasure for themselves in their new area.

"We've always loved old homes," says Carolyn, "and when we moved to Jefferson City we began looking for one to restore. But many of the older homes here were too dilapidated, or not for sale, or too far away from Rich's job. We just couldn't find what we wanted."

Their quest temporarily thwarted, the Greens built a new residence—a subdivision ranch-style house—and set about creating comfortable interiors with their many fine antique furnishings. But Rich and Carolyn kept hoping. Carolyn began to scour the countryside, searching for the elusive

◆ ◆ ◆

Missouri Dream

dream house. She mapped out possibilities with the help of a friend who had been a member of the Cole County Historical Society. Then one day she drove down into a rolling valley, 20 miles from Jefferson City, and saw a 2½-story Federal-style home built in 1872 of cut native limestone.

"I was enthralled," recalls Carolyn. "I wanted to find out everything about it." Carolyn was discouraged when she heard the house wasn't for sale. But hope springs eternal, and two months later she happened upon a classified listing that advertised a "2½-story rock home on 5 acres."

"That's all it said," says Carolyn, "but I called the Realtor and said I wanted to see the home *right now!*"

Happily, it was the same house. The property that surrounded it included woods, meadows, and many fine old stone outbuildings. Despite the work foretold by the unkept interiors, the Greens decided to purchase the place.

"We bought the house in December 1982 and moved in in January," says Carolyn. "It was terrible! The first two or three months were extremely rough. We

♦ ♦ ♦

Left: *Crimson wing chairs add a splash of bold color to Carolyn's scheme of checks and stripes in the family room. The tall cupboard in the corner is from Pennsylvania and dates to 1820. The Greens replaced the fireplace mantel and created the checkered fireboard.* Top: *In the entry a hanging rack is used to display a collection of Missouri homespun textiles.* Above: *"I love the warm, cozy look of blankets,"* says Carolyn, *"hanging, folded, or draped over whatever."*

Missouri Dream

lived in the kitchen and family rooms. The kids slept on two couches, and our bed was in there with the piano and TV. I'll never forget the day after we moved in. I was puttering around when Rich came down and said, 'It's just overwhelming! Will we ever get this done?' "

Thoroughly determined, however, the Greens began restoration work, gutting the interiors to prepare the house for modern living. Stud walls were built in front of the interior stone walls to carry new wiring and insulation. Wherever possible old trim was carefully removed, repaired, and replaced. Although Rich and Carolyn were reluctant to give up the house's original windows, their first winter convinced them to substitute new sash and insulating glass. The old tin roof was patched and repainted to ensure that Missouri's hard rains would not dampen the spirit of the restoration.

Each of the rooms was painstakingly repaired and finally anointed with special pieces from the Greens' collection of antiques. After years of love-filled labors, the Greens were successful in returning the old house

♦ ♦ ♦

Left: *A gentle repast of broccoli-and-cheese soup, blueberry muffins, and fresh fruit awaits hungry appetites in the dining area of the kitchen. The grain-painted settle is from New England and serves as extra seating.* Top: *Additional dining seating is available in the living room. Kansas City decorator and family friend Bruce Berstert painted the Windsor chairs.* Above: *Carolyn stores her yellowware and blue sponge pottery in an early 1800s step-back cupboard.*

Missouri Dream

to its handsome, original condition. They proudly dubbed their homestead Rock Enon Farm, after the name given to it by the first owner and builder, stonemason Louis Bruce.

"This house and its stone outbuildings are rare for this area of Missouri," remarks Carolyn. She established her antiques business in the old 1872 buggy shed across the road from the main house. Her shop specializes in painted country antiques and textiles.

"We lived in Jefferson City for three years," Carolyn continues, "and people would say to us, 'Why would you want to live out there?' Well, we just love it out here. We're not antisocial, but we love our old home and the land. I never want to live in town again!" □

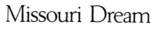

Above: *The master bedroom features an Ohio rope bed made in the mid-1800s. The chair next to the wardrobe comes from New England and reputedly served George Washington at the general's favorite Massachusetts inn.* Top left: *The Greens' daughter, Nicole, chose the woodwork color for her room and then added the comforter and rug.* Left: *Nicole shows off her collection of antique doll furniture.*

It's A Take!

By Ann Omvig Manternach. Produced by Estelle Bond Guralnick

When the call came, Country Home® *magazine took the challenge. We teamed up with television's* This Old House *to transform the interiors of Weatherbee Farm, a 200-year-old Massachusetts farmhouse, into a fresh and colorful home suited to an active young family. The result? It's a take!*

"Bob! Jean! Cut the discussion of the window treatment. You have to move over to the armoire faster."

From somewhere above a disembodied voice crackles curt instructions through a microphone. The recipients of these directions—Bob Vila, host of public television's popular home-renovation series *This Old House,* and Jean LemMon, editor of *Country Home* magazine— are being put through their paces. The two are practicing their on-camera cues for a TV tour of the circa-1785 Benjamin Weatherbee House, the

Right: *Newly restored by the crew of television's* This Old House, *the Benjamin Weatherbee House is located in Westwood, Massachusetts.* Above: *Prior to its restoration, the rambling farmhouse—built in 1785 and remodeled during the mid-1800s—was in sad need of repair.*

Photographs: William N. Hopkins, Hopkins Associates. Before photograph: Anthony Ching for WGBH. Interior design: Now and Then

Opposite top: *After seven months of intensive renovation, Bill, Cynthia, and Hannah Dromgoole are at home at last.*
Opposite bottom: *The watermelon-colored walls of the living room set the tone for color schemes throughout the house.*
Left: *Windows are draped with a length of semi-sheer cotton fabric in which rosettes have been gathered by hand, tied in place with twine, and hung from small nails.*
Below: *Bob Vila, host of public television's* This Old House, *and Jean LemMon, editor of* Country Home® *magazine, chat during the final taping of the Weatherbee Farm project.*

real star of the show's ninth season.

The man behind the voice? That's creator, producer, and director Russell Morash, whose proddings have shaped this award-winning how-to program.

Like everyone else on the set, Russ is anxious that all goes well. And it hasn't been easy. After days of prompting painters to finish that last bit of molding, moving and arranging furniture, uncrating and positioning props, and cleaning, cleaning, cleaning, we have readied Weatherbee Farm for its grand finale. Today is the day the *This Old House* crew tapes the 20th and final episode of the series segment that chronicles the restoration of this rambling farmhouse located in Westwood, Massachusetts.

Also anxious are homeowners Bill and Cynthia Dromgoole and their toddler daughter, Hannah. For them, the project began when they purchased the farmstead in 1986. Built 200 years earlier by young Benjamin Weatherbee (and remodeled in the mid-1800s), the house remained in the family through six generations until it passed into Bill and Cynthia's hands. Appropriately, the couple felt they weren't buying just a house, but a home with special historic and architectural history. Bill's career in rehabilitating old apartment buildings was evidence to local preservationists that these hands were capable ones.

Below: *Windows in the "beehive room"—the original kitchen with an unusual large chimney—are dressed with a delicate draping of dried herbs and flowers.*
Left: *This view of the beehive room before renovation shows the chimney and a doorway that has been removed.*
Opposite: *Cynthia's wedding china inspired the selection of flowered wallpaper in the dining room. A kilim rug repeats the floral motif; its black ground and a row of prints matted in black renew a living room accent.*

Before photograph: Brian Neudorfer for WGBH

Already into the early stages of consulting with
architect Mary Otis Stevens, the Dromgooles heard that
This Old House was searching for a historic home to
restore, one that would suit the needs of a young family.
They felt Weatherbee Farm fit the bill, and the series
staff agreed. "This project is exciting because it offers the
best of the old and the new," says Bob Vila. "It presents
the challenge of preserving the house's original integrity
as a piece of American history while sensitively
rebuilding a modern, functional space to suit the needs of
twentieth-century homeowners with a growing family."

When master carpenter Norm Abram and his *This Old
House* team arrived on the scene in June 1987, the couple
was elated. But today, not surprisingly, after months of
demolition, having the house in various states of repair
and reconstruction, and participating in assorted taping
sessions, Bill and Cynthia simply want to move in and
call Ben's old place "home."

It's A Take

Right: *A courtyard and herb garden welcome visitors to the kitchen/family room entrance.* Below: *The original one-story timber-framed ell at the back of the house was used as a storage shed. Though not salvageable, its shape provided a footprint for the new kitchen/family room addition.* Opposite top: *Jean and Bob filming in the kitchen.* Opposite bottom: *The efficient L-shaped kitchen features custom-made cabinets, a large island, up-to-date appliances, and a commercial range. The family room area is located behind the refrigerator wall.*

It was mid-September when program publicist Daphne Noyes put in the call: Would *Country Home* be interested in designing the interiors for the house? No question. The project was a natural for a magazine that promotes history, respect for craftsmanship, and an appreciation of American traditions; Jean flew to Boston to confer with Bill and Cynthia.

"They had a wonderful 200-year-old structure, but they are a young, active family and they didn't want to live in a museum," Jean later explained in an interview with *USA Today.* "They wanted an interior that was very livable, fresh, light, and lively—not stuffy at all."

Planning was coordinated with a local design team: Prudence Spencer, Linda Carbutt, and Kate Wharton of Now and Then located in Acton. Through meetings with Bill and Cynthia and endless phone calls to the *Country Home* magazine offices, they accomplished Jean's goal of "creating interiors that would be compatible with the age of the house while reflecting their [the Dromgooles'] casual and contemporary life-style."

Together the group tackled interior plans for the living room, dining room, a sitting room (now called the "beehive room" because it was the original kitchen and has an unusual, large chimney wall), the new kitchen/family room wing, and the nursery. New York designer Joe Ruggiero transformed the master suite on the second floor. (Two additional bedrooms and a main floor library await the Dromgooles' personal touches.)

Today, just three months after *Country Home* magazine received Daphne's call, our work draws to a close. Now the house must speak for itself. As the camera rolls and the taping begins, viewers discover that unexpected color rallies from every room—it's the primary element in the successful schemes the designers devised. "Though

Before photograph: Daphne B. Noyes for WGBH

Below: *Sliding glass doors and triangular windows in the gable wall of the vaulted family room provide a clear view of the old barn and new deck beyond. A casual sisal rug continues the indoor/outdoor theme, as does the floral skirted chair and the cushioned wicker rocker. A plump sofa complete with toss pillows provides a soft spot for morning coffee.*

Left: *The fabric's floral motif is repeated in stenciling that outlines the doors.*
Opposite top: *The sidewalls of the family area are covered with recycled barn board. A wall of French doors to the right of the painted farm table continues into the kitchen.*
Opposite bottom: *The gable wall of the old ell before it was dismantled and the new addition was constructed.*

the furniture's lines are traditional—Chippendale chairs, camelback sofa—the colors aren't," explains Jean. "We used a lot of painted finishes and high fashion colors on upholstered pieces. And we chose some brilliant wall colors as well."

Such vivid inspiration results from Cynthia's initial request: "I'd like the living room to be a little more formal than the rest of the house—but not standoffish."

The room concurs. Even though it's unusual to start a room scheme by choosing a color for the walls (typically the color is drawn from fabric, a rug, or perhaps a painted piece), "in this case," says designer Linda Carbutt, "the space just said, 'Paint me red.'"

Contrasting with the red, crisp white woodwork bespeaks the pretty windows and moldings. There's also a nice pattern mix in the upholstery: a linen print on the sofa, a tailored cotton stripe on the wing chair, and raw silk plaid for the cushion on the armchair. Cooling the warm scheme is a creamy beige-on-white wool rug.

Cynthia's English bone china sets the stage for the dining room. Bordered with small red flowers that echo the living room wall color, the china inspired the

Before photograph: Daphne B. Noyes for WGBH

Opposite top: *The master bedroom's subtle color scheme provides a refreshing retreat for Bill and Cynthia. A mix of floral fabrics on bed, canopy, and window echo colors found elsewhere in the house. Simple window treatments are made by gathering a king-size ruffled pillow sham at each end and tying it with cording.*
Opposite bottom: *Faux painting emphasizes the architectural details.*
Below: *Buff-colored tile matches the wallpaper in the master bath.*
Left: *The master bedroom prior to painting and papering.*

Before photograph: Brian Neudorfer for WGBH. Master suite interior design: Joe Ruggiero, WestPoint Pepperell

selection of floral wallpaper on a white ground. A
matching border, used at chair rail height, adds
architectural interest to the room.

Because Cynthia and Bill want a "light, happy look"
for the room, a mix of woods is used to contrast with the
dark stain of the fireplace mantel. "We went for a real
mix of updated English and French in the furnishings,"
says Linda, referring to the Chippendale-style chairs, the
hutch, and the painted dining table.

Moving into less formal areas of the house, the
designers created a family haven in the beehive room. "I
see this as a nighttime room," says Cynthia of the casual
sitting area, "a place to feel cozy and enveloped." The
colors—blue for the walls and tomato-red woodwork—are
drawn from the Dromgooles' Oriental rug and are rich
enough to warm the room's north light.

Opening onto the beehive room is Weatherbee Farm's
new addition: a combined kitchen, work space, and
family room with eating area. A bank of French doors
and a glass wall at the family room end fill the airy room
with abundant light. To capitalize on this indoor/outdoor
aspect, the windows are left uncovered; a stencil

Right: *Little Hannah plays in her bright and cheery new nursery. Covering the white-painted floor is a red and white striped dhurrie rug trimmed with a border of hearts. At the window, a puffy balloon shade is trimmed with satin ribbons.*

Benjamin Weatherbee House 1785

pattern drawn from the green-and-rose floral fabric used in the room outlines both windows and doors.

Upstairs, whispers of "cozy retreat" slip from the master suite. Here designer Joe Ruggiero, a master at combining fabrics, used bed linens as the starting point for his restful neutral color scheme. For the canopy bed he chose coordinated floral designs in shades of rose and green; a small-scale buff-colored wallpaper serves as the backdrop. "This understated allover wallpaper pattern works beautifully with larger florals and checks," he says. Painted surfaces—from buff-colored floor to faux-marbled woodwork—comfortably coexist with a combination of new wood furniture and the Dromgooles' antiques.

Color again asserts itself as red reappears in Hannah's nursery, *above*. According to the plan, Cynthia wants an "androgynous nursery, not one that said boy or girl." She also has in mind that the small room, located next to the master bedroom, might one day be used as a sitting room or office. To accommodate that, a patterned wallpaper in pink and blue on red provides a cheerful background that can change roles.

Camera and sound crews pack their equipment as production assistants scurry to load the vans. Final good-byes are said and the doors close. Standing proud at drive's edge, Benjamin Weatherbee's house seems to heave a sigh as silence finally descends on the old farmstead. Though it's weathered tough times in the past 200 years—and during the last seven months—it looks expectantly to the future with a fresh face. □

TRAVELER in TIME

The transformation of a Minnesota tract home

By Linda Joan Smith

Time continues apace with the rest of the world on Faribault, Minnesota's, Prairie Avenue. The street is paved, the lawns are mowed, and there's a car in every garage. Kids ride bikes, joggers pass, dogs are walked, and mail delivered. The year is 1988, and not a single passerby would doubt it. Even the houses are chronologically correct—not a fanlight nor portico among them to connect them to the past.

Steve and Bobbie Bollenbach's small house fits right in among its suburban neighbors. There are rustic touches—a plank door, a split-rail fence—to set it apart, but otherwise it is quiet and subdued, making no particular statement to the world. Just one house among many, its street facade gives little hint of what awaits inside.

Step beyond that plank door, however, and the din of the modern world fades eerily into the distance. Light grows soft, colors warm, and time spins away into a thin thread that forgets the present and stretches back into the past. What is the year now?

Top left: *Inside Steve and Bobbie Bollenbach's modest Minnesota ranch home, the clock has been turned back more than 100 years.* Left: *Primitive antiques and domestic goods—baskets, pottery, pewter, and textiles—fill each room of the small house.*

Photographs: William N. Hopkins, Hopkins Associates. Produced by Patricia Carpenter

Traveler in Time

1880? 1870? The date itself does not matter. We have slipped into a pocket of the past that we thought was lost forever, and it feels like home.

This passage back in time feels a bit like magic, and in truth, it is a masterful sleight of hand. The magician is 26-year-old Bobbie, who transformed the interior of this seven-year-old tract house into a 19th-century haven using little more than a hammer, nails, and her imagination.

About four years ago Bobbie started reading about antiques and period styles. "As I grew in my knowledge, I grew in my taste," she says. As her tastes developed, Bobbie made changes in the house. At first it was just the addition of a few antiques. But the tract house interior, with its plain walls, hollow-core doors, and carpeted floors, didn't provide the period feeling Bobbie wanted. So, she started adding: an old door here, a shutter there.

As she progressed, she found it was easier and far less expensive to translate her ideas into reality than to hire someone else to do the job. "I can't afford to have things done for me, and if I could, I'm afraid they wouldn't do it the way I'd want it done," she explains. "I want a primitive, homey, handmade look—not something professional."

Above: *Steve and Bobbie with sons Chris and Nick, ages 9 and 5, in the dining room.*
Right: *Bobbie worked magic in the living room by putting split logs right over the drywall, then mortaring between them for a log-cabin look.*
Below: *Painted furniture holds a special place in Bobbie's heart.*

Traveler in Time

Pleased with the results of her initial handiwork, Bobbie grew bold. Over the last three years she has coaxed the entire house, which began life quite devoid of vintage character, through an amazing metamorphosis.

In the living room (and throughout the house), she pulled up the carpet and replaced it with wide pine floorboards that date from the 1860s. To mimic the look of a log homestead, Bobbie screwed sections of roughly split logs to the studs of the walls right over the drywall, then filled the large gaps between them with mortar. Even the fact that the house had no fireplace didn't daunt Bobbie's building spirit; she simply constructed a nonworking fireplace, complete with an antique mantel and flanking chimney cupboards, along one living room wall.

The modern windows of the house provided Bobbie with a dilemma. Should she spend the money to replace them or make do with what she had? In the end, she compromised. Throughout most of the house, Bobbie disguised the modern windows with rustic wood frames, then softened them with curtains of homespun tied back with string. A large picture window in the living room seemed particularly jarring as

Above: *Bobbie constructed a board-and-batten door to replace the original storm door.*
Left: *A painted chest with 35 drawers makes an eye-catching buffet for the dining room.*
Below: *The kitchen originally was open to the dining room, but the Bollenbachs enclosed it for a more old-fashioned look.*

Traveler in Time

the room slipped further back in time, so she replaced it with an old multi-paned window flanked by bead-board shutters.

Along with the windows, the original closets struck an anachronistic note. To make over the hallway closet, *right,* Bobbie removed the door and tucked the bottom of an old cupboard into the space. In the upper portion of the closet she installed shelves, then added glass doors she found at a flea market.

To rework a closet for her sons, Nick and Chris, ages 5 and 9, Bobbie removed the closet doors and pushed a dresser into one side of the lower space, *below.* Bead-board doors cover the top half of the closet; steps along one side help the boys reach their clothes and the television set.

Rough-hewn logs provide the homestead feeling Bobbie wants in the living room, but for the other rooms she chose a variety of wall treatments. In the dining room and kitchen she installed wide boards of knotty pine, and the master bedroom received a bead-board wainscot. In her sons' room, *right,* Bobbie nailed random lengths of narrow board horizontally, then painted them for a whitewash effect.

Above: *A narrow hall closet became an attractive display case for collectibles, thanks to Bobbie's carpentry skills.* Right: *The boys' cheerful room is filled with the toys of childhood past.* Below: *Chris and Nick's closet, once fitted with bifold doors, now blends in with its old-time surroundings.*

Traveler in Time

Steve helped with some cleanup work when time off from his job allowed, but otherwise Bobbie did all of the reconstruction and decorating work. "I guess my dad was always handy—he was always making things—and I just grew up with that ability," says Bobbie.

Six years ago, when the Bollenbachs bought the just-built house, Bobbie never envisioned that it would one day look like a home from a century past. Since that time, she, too, has undergone a transformation. "I grew up around antiques because my parents were into them," Bobbie says. "But I never appreciated them. In fact, I told my dad, when I was about ten, that I was never going to have all this old junk in my house. I was so sick of old dressers that didn't open quite right."

Now, there isn't a corner of the house that doesn't show Bobbie's transforming touch and her recently awakened love of the previous century.

"This place isn't exactly professional," she says. "But this is the way the early settlers did it. That's what I like about country living—you make the stuff yourself, and you're proud of it."

In keeping with Bobbie's pioneering spirit, she and Steve eventually hope to build a place of their own from the ground up. And if Bobbie has her way, it will be a log house built with the remnants of early homesteads and evocative of times long past. Her hammer hand is at the ready . . . . □

Below: *A bead-board wainscot and ceiling, painted a warm ocher hue, gives the Bollenbachs' bedroom the air of a 19th-century farmhouse. The floorboards, which Bobbie installed and sanded by hand, came from an 1860s country church.*

December

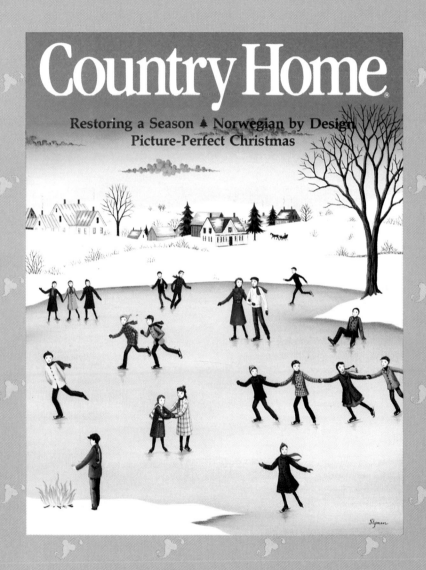

Country Home

Restoring a Season ♣ Norwegian by Design
Picture-Perfect Christmas

RESTORING a SEASON

By Marcia King

A light snow begins as dusk falls. Inside the large saltbox home on the hill, Duane Boyd lights the candles in the chandelier while his wife, Mary Margaret, makes supper in the keeping room fireplace. The room glows with soft light, illuminated only by the hearth fire and the candles flickering in holiday arrangements of grapes and fir sprigs.

Top: *Duane and Mary Margaret Boyd eagerly await Christmas with Erin and Trevor, the younger two of the couple's four children.* Above: *This newly built Ohio home was inspired by the 1700s saltbox homes of New England.* Right: *An old-fashioned Frazier fir in the living room is trimmed with cranberries, apples, and home-baked gingerbread cookies.*

132   Photographs: Al Teufen. Produced by Ann Omvig Manternach

After a candlelight supper with their children, Erin and Trevor, the couple retires to the living room, and the Currier and Ives-like scene fades as Duane opens the door of a large built-in antique cupboard and pops a cassette into the VCR. "We may be purists," laughs Mary Margaret, "but we're not extremists!"

Specifically, she is referring to their new home, a reproduction of a 1700s New England saltbox. Besides the lap

siding, central chimney, and long, sloping roof which define the saltbox style, the Boyds' home has thick interior walls, wide hallways, and old salvaged woodwork and beams.

Located in a suburb of Canton, Ohio, the home took two years—1984 to 1986—to finish. Construction was under the strict supervision of Duane, who served as the contractor.

"We couldn't find a house plan that really met our needs," he says. "So we

Left: *Woodwork in the living room was salvaged from an 1840s Ohio mansion and recut by Duane to fit their new home. The detailing of the wood lends a formal look to the room and is complemented by simple but classic window treatments and furnishings.*

Top: *Apples, oranges, lemons, and pineapples are used in Williamsburg-style arrangements on the living room mantel and throughout the house.* Above: *A mural in the style of Rufus Porter—an itinerant painter in New England during the early 1800s—decorates the dining room.*

135

bought plan books, found a center chimney location, and we literally designed the house. There were only rough drawings."

In addition, Duane cleaned and fit woodwork from an abandoned 1840s mansion into the home. The Boyds purchased the interior trim and, in the January cold, ripped out all of the woodwork. Their treasure trove included flared Egyptian-style door and window molding, decorated jambs, mantels, cupboards, floating panels, doors, mopboards, chair rail, and a cherry staircase. They even saved square nails to hang things on. The kitchen beams were salvaged from a corncrib adjacent to the mansion;

those in the keeping room from another early house.

To install the wide old doors and jambs, the Boyds made some interior walls thicker by using 2×8s, imparting a solidness rarely found in new homes. Hallways are extra-wide—enough so to hold pieces of furniture. The size, says Mary Margaret, is an Ohio variant. "When we took the wood out of the old house, it had a big foyer. It seemed appropriate to continue it." As for wide hallways, she believes that "for the aesthetics of decorating, you can't beat it."

Mary Margaret was as serious about properly dressing their home as Duane was about correct

architectural elements. The look she sought was that of a middle-class, early 1800s home. "It's high country," she says. "Not formal, not real primitive. A little bit 'up.' "

Furniture is almost exclusively pre-Civil War with an emphasis on painted pieces. "The wealthy used wallpapers and finer woods. Those of lesser means used painted woods and murals," she says. To flatter the painted woods, the walls are left off-white. Exceptions are

Left: *The keeping room at the rear of the house combines this sitting area, a kitchen work space to the right, and a dining area to the left.* Above: *The green-and-mustard-painted cupboard in the keeping room belonged to Erin and*

Trevor's great-grandparents. Although the case, drawers, and doors are original, the glass had been broken. Duane located old glass, had mullions made for the door inserts, and had the entire piece repainted.

the mural in the dining room and a stencil border in the keeping room. Both are copies of designs by Rufus Porter, an itinerant New England painter of the 1830s and '40s.

Mary Margaret uses smaller items to complete the decor: old baskets, stoneware, pewter, cooking utensils, quilts, dipped candles, and dishes. Red- and yellowware are used for baking; blue feather-edge dishes for special dinners. An apothecary chest stores herbs; an old barrel holds apples. "Everything that is bought has a function," she says. "That's my one criterion when I buy antiques."

The Boyds also strive for a lean, uncluttered look, which includes their Christmas decor as well. Because homes weren't heavily decorated until the Victorian Era, they prefer simple ornaments. Says Mary Margaret of the holiday trims they use, "They're Williamsburg arrangements: a lot of fruit, greens, and nuts. We use a Frazier fir—an old type of tree—in the living room. It looks stark, spindly almost. Wonderful to hang things on."

Incredibly, only six years ago, neither Duane nor Mary Margaret had much awareness in antiques or historic architecture. Even more fantastic, all their antiques were collected in a mere four years.

Duane had enjoyed Civil

War history (he now has his own Civil War room) while Mary Margaret had an undeveloped, vaguely defined interest in country and colonial furnishings. After they met and married in 1983, the couple combined those interests and together discovered a world of historic customs, period furnishings, and pre-Civil War architecture.

They sold their contemporary colonial two-story, got rid of virtually all their furnishings, and

Left: *An addition at the rear of the house would probably have been a summer kitchen in a New England saltbox. The Boyds opted to make the brick-floored space a sunny breakfast spot furnished with primitive pieces.*

Above: *Woodwork in the kitchen is made from new wood but was beaded by Duane with an antique beading plane to mimic the older woodwork used elsewhere in the house. The cabinet at right disguises the refrigerator.*

started going on buying trips to New England.

"We purchased a lot of books," says Mary Margaret, "did a lot of reading, talking, and attending museums."

Because of her love for collecting, a small antiques business has evolved as a hobby. Her furnishings are her inventory. Mary Margaret buys what she and Duane like, introduces it into their home, and keeps it until they find a piece that pleases them even more. "It's a

wonderful business," she says. "How else can you keep changing your furnishings? A year from now, our house may not look the same."

But one thing will remain the same. No matter which furniture comes and goes, the Boyd home will always reflect the classic good looks and middle-class comfort of the typical American family—1800s style. □

Marcia King, a free-lance writer from Ohio, specializes in travel writing, historical home features, and personality profiles.

Left: *The master bedroom, located just above the living room, contains one of the house's three fireplaces. Floors in this room, as throughout the house, are constructed of new random-width tongue-and-groove poplar. The king-size bed, Duane's concession to comfort, is a reproduction.*

Top: *Duane's Civil War room is furnished with period pieces. Because of his enthusiasm he continually searches for more artifacts and is involved in a military reenactment group.*
Above: *Daughter Erin's room is furnished with antique pieces and old-fashioned toys.*

NORWEGIAN by DESIGN

By Deborah Hufford
Produced by Ann Omvig Manternach

Iowans Cathy and Dennis Barber capture a yuletide spirit that harks back to Christmases celebrated long ago in a faraway land.

On a snowy evening in Waterloo, Iowa, indigo shadows chase the velvet twilight down a treelined street. It's late December and night falls early. But on Graceline Boulevard, nearly 100 lanterns bedecked with bows and evergreen shrug off winter's darkness.

"Lighting the lanterns is a special neighborhood tradition that's been carried on for the last twenty-five years. It really captures the spirit of Christmas—of sharing," says Cathy Barber, who lives in a colonial-style home on Graceline with her husband, Dennis, a mechanical engineer, and their two small children, Julie and Christopher. "Even when a home is sold, the lanterns stay with the house for the next owners."

The festive lighting is one of the many yuletide traditions the

Right: Dennis and Cathy Barber's home graces a picturesque street in Waterloo, Iowa. The neighborhood celebrates Christmas by hanging a red lantern from each tree. Above: On Christmas Eve, the Barber family sets out a gingerbread offering for Santa Claus. Surrounding Santa's snack are some of the family's cherished Norwegian heirlooms and other antiques: A table runner made of hardanger embroidery, Dennis' grandparents' photo album, and turn-of-the-century Christmas cards.

142

Photographs: William N. Hopkins, Hopkins Associates

NORWEGIAN
by DESIGN

Barbers enjoy. During the holiday season, their home glows with a yuletide spirit that harks back to Christmases that were celebrated long ago in a faraway land.

"My family has a Norwegian

Left: *During the Christmas season, Cathy and Dennis and their children, Julie and Christopher, celebrate with Scandinavian flair.* Right: *The Barbers' rich Norwegian heritage inspires the simple holiday trimmings in the living room. The couch is an 1830s pullout bed that was purchased near the Norwegian-Swedish border.* Below: *This small Norwegian square-nailed cabinet brims with family relics.*

background," says Dennis, "and we have a lot of family heirlooms and Scandinavian antiques. The atmosphere lends itself to an old-fashioned kind of Christmas."

On Christmas Eve, garlands of evergreen drape across the fireplace mantel and trim the staircase. A fire crackles on the hearth, and candles adorn the Christmas tree. Dried apple rings and Scandinavian straw ornaments hang from the tree's sparse branches. Presents wrapped in brown sacking and calico ribbon are tucked beneath the tree. Heirloom toys take an honored place beside the gifts each year. One of these antiques—a hand-hewn cradle—holds a child's doll. The cradle rocked generations of babies before the Barbers used it for their son, Christopher.

"The primitive Christmas gifts that poor Norwegian immigrant farmers made by hand make a sharp contrast with the abundance of modern holiday fare," Dennis says. "These simple handmade items are

NORWEGIAN
by DESIGN

still the most treasured gifts. They bring us as much pleasure as they would have in a simple log cabin a hundred years ago."

The Barbers' extensive collection of family heirlooms and primitive Norwegian and Swedish antiques is

Left: *An 1801 Swedish linen cabinet with exquisite geometric and floral patterns dominates the dining room. A handmade yule tree, decorated with gingerbread ornaments, reflects the simplicity of Scandinavian design.* Right: *Paper silhouettes of Christmas scenes parade across the cupboards of this 1800s Norwegian pine cabinet. The antique Norwegian ale bowl on top of the cabinet is a prized possession in the Barber household.*

set against a backdrop of crisp white walls and refinished wood floors. Some of the walls and floors are embellished with stenciled borders and decorative scenes, which Cathy created from paper sacks.

The effect is typically Scandinavian, a mix of Spartan charm with subtle touches of ornamentation.

"When we bought the house seven years ago, it was worse than ugly," says Dennis. "It probably hadn't been redecorated since it was built in the 1930s. There were hideous wallpapers—forest green with color-coordinated patterns that alternated between huge florals and stripes. The ceilings and carpets were pink."

The garish wallpaper and gaudy carpeting were stripped, revealing the interior's original textures. "The whole house took five years to finally finish. It's been a real artistic outlet for us," Cathy says. "Most of our antiques have been purchased since we moved in."

Some of the Barbers' acquisitions

Left: *The upstairs master bedroom boasts a charming mix of antiques and family nostalgia. The bright starburst quilt on the wall and the appliquéd summer bedcover were purchased locally. Vintage nightclothes hang above the bed, including Cathy's grandmother's christening gown, also used in daughter Julie's baptism.* Right: *An inviting alcove off the master bedroom harbors a small tree surrounded by antique toys. Cathy's stenciling above the archway imitates delicate rosemaling.*

NORWEGIAN
by DESIGN

hold uncanny links to their ancestors. Cathy found one trunk in a Minnesota antiques store. A family name engraved on the trunk led to the discovery that the chest once belonged to Dennis' great-great-uncle. "We asked the dealer where

he bought it," says Cathy, "and he described a farm, which turned out to be the family homestead."

Another trunk, purchased at a local antiques store, revealed a similar quirk of fate. Painted on the outside of the trunk was another family name, along with shipping instructions that routed the trunk from Germany, through New York, to its final destination in Waverly, Iowa. "Cathy's grandmother came to our house and took one look at the chest and said, 'Where did you get Uncle Herman's trunk!' We couldn't believe it."

Other prized household possessions are two ale bowls. One bowl dates back to the 18th century. Another one, dated 1812, bears the whimsical

NORWEGIAN
by DESIGN

prose, "I am a bowl so fair and fine, If only filled with brandy wine."

The Barbers proudly display one of the ale bowls atop a Norwegian pine cabinet in the dining room. Across the room, a glazed crock anchors a homemade Scandinavian yule tree made of raw pine lath. Simple

Above: *Bursting with antique toys and Christmas cutouts, Julie's bedroom is a child's delight.* Left: *The chenille bedspread and star quilt were* *purchased at an antiques store.* Below: *Dressed in red flannel pajamas, Christopher hears a bedtime story. Cathy stenciled his bedroom walls and* *floors using her own designs cut from paper bags. Miniatures of homes on Graceline Boulevard, made by Cathy and Dennis, perch on the windowsill.*

gingerbread ornaments hang from its modest branches. On top, a tuft of evergreen and a shiny red apple serve as the star.

Each year, Cathy melds old family customs with new traditions when preparing for the holidays. The warm, sweet aroma of her baking wafts from the kitchen weeks before Christmas. She bakes her favorite holiday treats—kringla and sugar cookies—using old family recipes. Her daughter Julie's handmade decorations hang beside Victorian scrap ornaments.

"When readying for Christmas, I think of the many generations and many Christmases that are represented here," says Cathy. "I enjoy the thought that maybe one hundred years from now someone might be hanging one of Julie's ornaments on their tree and feel the pleasure of a happy Christmas long ago." □

Picture-Perfect
Christmas

By Candace Ord Manroe
Produced by Estelle Bond Guralnick

589

Photographs: Bill Stites

151

Picture-Perfect Christmas

If objects had spirits, illustrator Hilary Newby's home and her art would be kindred. Wrapped doorstep-deep in snow, its lights winking invitingly, the Norwell, Massachusetts, farmhouse she shares with husband Mark and their two small children hugs the heart like a second chance at innocence: simple, happy. Not coincidentally, the watercolor-and-pencil mice and bunnies that cavort in Hilary's illustrations stir a similar emotion, warm and fuzzy.

This snug melding of form and function, of persons and place, is what sets the Newby home apart—and seldom does that fit seem more inviting than at Christmas.

The Newbys, after a frustrating year of searching, knew when they first saw the circa-1840 clapboard home that it was the one.

Left: *Antique oak and bentwood create dining room warmth.* Bottom: *Hilary and Mark Newby observe Christmas with their children, Peter and Willow, in the living room.* Above: *Hilary made the Advent calendar.* Below: *Santa mouse is Hilary's design.*

Picture-Perfect Christmas

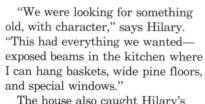

Above: *Hilary, whose parents are artists, designs for the national card company she started in her home.* Below: *Bunnies dominate her art.* Bottom: *Open shelves create a casual kitchen.* Right: *Timeless wicker and old beams grace the restored barn's living area.*

"We were looking for something old, with character," says Hilary. "This had everything we wanted—exposed beams in the kitchen where I can hang baskets, wide pine floors, and special windows."

The house also caught Hilary's artistic eye as a good place to pursue her work as a free-lance illustrator. Its serene, spacious studio, which Mark and Hilary later would graft from the down-at-the-heels attached barn, would be just the motivation Hilary needed to launch her own illustrated-cards business, Hilary Designs. And better still, except for the barn, the house already was restored.

The location, a scant half-hour's drive from Boston, was another plus:

Picture-Perfect Christmas

Right: *Renovated, the light-bathed barn loft makes an ideal studio for Hilary (see detail of her work,* below). Bottom: *Carpenter Walter Paal, aided by Michael Bastoni in the barn restoration, avoided metal spiral stairs by creating his own space-saving design in wood.*

The Newbys can nurture son Peter, 5, and daughter Willow, 3, on the wholesome staples of rural life, while still enjoying an occasional slice of rich urban pie themselves.

During their seven years here, the Newbys have imprinted the home with fresh paint, a picket fence, family antiques, and country finds from their own haunts at auctions and shops. The result is an easy livability, tasteful and unstrained.

Nowhere is that warmth more apparent than in the barn. Mark saw its potential immediately: "It was ready to fall in, but I envisioned it as a large, open living space—something that had always appealed to me. It was just a question of when we would get around to restoring it."

When he wasn't working at his own electronics-sales business or building houses for the less fortunate as a Habitat for Humanity volunteer, Mark aided carpenters Walter Paal and Michael Bastoni in the redo, using old beams for authenticity.

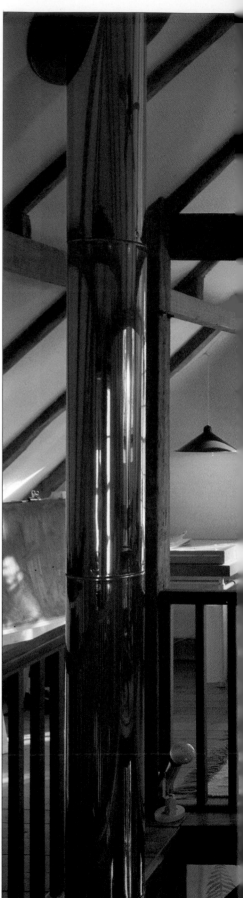

Picture-Perfect Christmas

Above: *Peter inspects a living room nativity.* Right: *His bedroom features a handcrafted bed and toys.* Below: *Victoriana and a dress dummy soften the master bedroom.*

The barn is the hub of the house every day, but especially at Christmas; then, it beams. "We all get involved with decorating," Hilary says, "and everything really comes alive."

Christmas music provides a soothing backdrop as doors are swagged and wreathed with aromatic greens, and chestnuts and other natural bounty are lavished atop furnishings.

Christmas morning, the festivities culminate in the barn, where presents are opened beneath the old-fashioned tree. In this good-feeling farmhouse, the childlike magic of Christmas is happily at home. □

Index

Page numbers in **bold** type refer to photographs or to illustrated text.

Have BETTER HOMES AND GARDENS®
magazine delivered to your door. For
information, write to:
MR. ROBERT AUSTIN
P.O. BOX 4536
DES MOINES, IA 50336